CAGE FIGHT

The Hoover Institution gratefully acknowledges the following individuals and foundations for their significant support of the ROLE OF MILITARY HISTORY IN CONTEMPORARY CONFLICT WORKING GROUP *and this publication:*

Martin Anderson

The Lynde & Harry Bradley Foundation

Pilar and Lew Davies

William L. Edwards and Marienne Emblad

Patrick and Rachel English

The Bertha and John Garabedian
Charitable Foundation

James and Daphne Jameson

Jennifer L. "Jenji" Mercer

Rebekah Mercer

Roger and Martha Mertz

Jeremiah Milbank III

Sarah Scaife Foundation

Victor S. Trione

CAGE FIGHT

Civilian and Democratic Pressures on Military Conflicts and Foreign Policy

Edited by Bruce S. Thornton

HOOVER INSTITUTION PRESS

STANFORD UNIVERSITY   STANFORD, CALIFORNIA

With its eminent scholars and world-renowned library and archives, the Hoover Institution seeks to improve the human condition by advancing ideas that promote economic opportunity and prosperity, while securing and safeguarding peace for America and all mankind. The views expressed in its publications are entirely those of the authors and do not necessarily reflect the views of the staff, officers, or Board of Overseers of the Hoover Institution.

hoover.org

Hoover Institution Press Publication No. 728

Hoover Institution at Leland Stanford Junior University,
Stanford, California 94305-6003

First printing 2023
29 28 27 26 25 24 23   7 6 5 4 3 2 1

Manufactured in the United States of America
Printed on acid-free, archival-quality paper

Library of Congress Control Number: 2022946964

ISBN 978-0-8179-2544-4 (cloth)
ISBN 978-0-8179-2546-8 (epub)
ISBN 978-0-8179-2548-2 (PDF)

CONTENTS

INTRODUCTION

Bruce S. Thornton

In *The Gathering Storm*, Winston Churchill in cataloguing the causes of World War II listed "the structure and habits of democratic States," which "lack those elements of persistence and conviction which alone can give security to humble masses," and pointed out "how, even in matters of self-preservation, no policy is pursued for even ten or fifteen years at a time."[1] From the birth of democracy in ancient Athens, the political institutions that protect the freedom and rights of citizens have also been potentially dangerous in times of war by complicating and interfering with the policies and decisions that during a conflict require swift execution, decisiveness, and persistence.

The "structure and habits" Churchill notes include regularly scheduled elections, by which the citizens hold their elected leaders accountable; the right of all citizens to speak openly and freely on all matters, including the conduct of foreign policy and the management of war; and the voicing of dissent against the war itself and the reasons for conducting it. Most important, the military establishment and war are subordinated to the civilian institutions and offices accountable to the citizens through elections.

REGULARLY SCHEDULED ELECTIONS

As Churchill suggested above, regularly scheduled elections, in the United States held every two years, make long-term military strategies vulnerable to the shifting moods of the electorate expressed in frequent turnovers in Congress and the presidency. On the other hand, this critical instrument of political accountability can also change a dangerous course.

The iconic example in recent American history is the election of Ronald Reagan in 1980. His predecessor, Jimmy Carter, elected after the disastrous abandonment of Vietnam, counseled that we should get over our "inordinate fear of communism" and prioritize human rights in our foreign policy rather than containing and pushing back on the Soviet Union's adventurism in Latin America, Afghanistan, and Central Africa. Reagan in contrast announced that it was "Morning in America" exuded confidence and faith in America's goodness, increased the military budget, pushed back against Soviet interventions in Latin America, and summed up his strategy for dealing with the Soviet Union as, "We win, they lose," thus abandoning the prior policies of "peaceful coexistence" and "détente."

Similarly, Donald Trump's election in 2016 led to a change in military policy from Barack Obama's foreign policy of retreat, diplomatic engagement, and "leading from behind." Obama had sought a "reset" with Russia, with promises of "flexibility" made indirectly to Vladimir Putin; subsequently abandoned antimissile batteries for Poland and the Czech Republic and Javelin antitank weapons for Ukraine; and in October 2011 withdrew our forces from Iraq. This latter move created a power vacuum quickly filled by Iran, ISIS, and other jihadist organizations, and exacerbated the brutal civil war in Syria by enabling Russia and Iran to take a larger role in that conflict and the wider region. Trump also left the Joint Comprehensive Plan of Action agreement Obama signed with Iran that aimed at slowing down, not stopping, its march to nuclear weapons capability.

But disgruntled voters don't always express their impatience with policy in such starkly partisan terms. Responding to voter displeasure, Donald Trump had campaigned against the unpopular "endless wars" in Afghanistan and Iraq and near the end of his term had negotiated with the Taliban for the withdrawal of US troops from

Afghanistan. The Biden administration had campaigned on the same aim, which as we know was disastrously carried out in 2021. Biden's withdrawal resulted in the loss of thirteen American troops and the abandonment of hundreds of American citizens as well as Afghans who had worked for the US authorities. Left behind as well were billions of dollars' worth of weapons and other materiel.

We'll never know if Trump's withdrawal would have been less disastrous. But the point is that some policies are disliked by voters from both parties, which compels Democrat and Republican candidates to promise to address voters' concerns, even if it compromises long-term strategies for short-term political gain. As the saying goes, the enemy has a metaphorical vote; but the citizens have a literal one that can end a politician's career or one party's control of government.

FREE SPEECH AND DISSENT

Relations between civilian governments and the military have often been contentious, especially over the management of a conflict, its tactics, and its purposes. The constitutional right to free speech allows citizens to criticize and protest publicly how a war is conducted, which complicates military planning, and puts pressure on the elected officials who are held accountable on election day for setbacks and failures.

Since the sixties and the contentious, divisive war in Vietnam, antiwar organizations have proliferated, and protests have accompanied every conflict since then. These constitutionally protected events obviously complicate the prosecution of the war and bolster the enemy's morale even as they intimidated presidents, members of Congress, and aspirants to those offices facing an election. Such demonstrations, extensively covered by the media, also impact domestic politics such as police tactics for controlling crime and sentencing guidelines for convicted criminals.

A good example is the antiwar protests over the 2003 war in Iraq. The 2004 presidential primary overlapped with the violent guerrilla resistance to the American occupation in Iraq. Democratic Vermont governor Howard Dean used the protests to mount a digital grass-roots campaign for the nomination and gained surprising traction and support. Dean's brief success spooked the frontrunners for the nomination, Senators John Kerry, John Edwards, and Hillary Clinton, who reversed their support for the war, even though they had earlier voted for the Authorization for Use of Military Force that sanctioned it, based on the same intelligence regarding weapons of mass destruction (WMDs) that was one of George Bush's predicates for the war. For the Democrats, opposition to the war became an important plank in the party's platform and eventually candidate John Kerry's campaign.

Barack Obama's 2008 presidential campaign likewise incorporated the antiwar movement's interpretation of the Iraq War as unnecessary and based on false, if not manufactured, evidence for Saddam Hussein's WMDs. By then voters were growing tired of the occupations of Afghanistan and Iraq, both of which were still troubled by violence and seemingly making little progress toward fulfilling Bush's aim to create liberal democracies in nations culturally unsuited for Western political ideals.

In 2007, with the antiwar movement still active, then senator Obama responded to the "surge" of troops to Iraq, which eventually reduced the violence, by calling it a "reckless escalation," and introduced legislation to remove all US combat forces by March 31, 2008.[2] Obama's presidential campaign likewise highlighted the war in Iraq as predicated on fabricated intelligence and dubious strategic aims.

Which brings us back to the eventual disastrous withdrawal of US troops from Afghanistan by the Biden administration in 2021, following the terms set by his predecessor. Such disastrous fallout, intended or not, from people exercising their First Amendment rights is the price we pay for the foundational freedom of our political order.

CIVILIAN CONTROL OF THE MILITARY

The subordination of the military establishment to civilian power is critical for protecting the freedom of the people. In the United States, this is achieved by Congress possessing the power to declare war, and by the president serving as commander in chief of the US military even if he does not necessarily have any military experience or training. These provisions give the people the power through representatives they elect to make war, and hold the military accountable for how it conducts it.

These guardrails were designed to protect people and their freedoms from the national institution that comprises those who are trained in warfare and have access to the materiel for making war. The Founders checked military institutions by elected officeholders because European history was replete with examples of powerful military leaders, autocrats, and kings who commanded armies without accountability to the people or who often turned against civilian political institutions in order to create some form of tyranny. Moreover, the centuries of chronic European warfare waged by monarchs commanding large armies—especially the French and Indian War or Seven Years' War (1754–63), in which the colonies' militias fought—typified the abuse of power and deadly destruction that were endemic in European monarchies commanding huge armies of subjects who had no say about what they were risking their lives for.

During the revolutionary and founding period, however, one of the premier historical examples of this danger was Julius Caesar, who abused the terms of his *imperium*, the right granted by the Roman Senate to wage war on behalf of the Republic, by marching his legions into the city of Rome and its territory in violation of the law, thus becoming a tyrant not accountable to the people or the Senate. For the American colonists chafing against the governance of the British parliament and king, those Romans who resisted Caesar by fighting against him like Cato the Younger, or participating in his assassination like Brutus, were the glorious embodiments of the defense of freedom against tyranny. Perhaps the most popular literary work during this period was English playwright Joseph Addison's tragedy *Cato* (1712), which glorifies Cato's suicide after Caesar's victory over Pompey at Pharsalus. Cato had refused to accept Caesar's offer of clemency.

This distrust of the military and fear of "standing armies" has been a perennial feature of American history. But the Cold War struggle between two nuclear-armed superpowers could not be settled by direct battles, given the risk of mutually assured destruction in such a confrontation. Proxy duels between each side's clients, such as the wars in Korea and Vietnam, punctuated the decades-long stalemate. The strategy of containment on a global scale required a much larger military and more sophisticated materiel.

This strategy also necessitated a permanent security and defense establishment during the Cold War that fed off this traditional suspicion and distrust of standing armies as expressed in novels and movies like *Seven Days in May* (1964), in which military leaders plot to overthrow the president, and *The Manchurian Candidate* (1962), about a POW during the Korean War who is brainwashed to assassinate a presidential candidate so a communist stooge can replace him.

Also, the defense budget now took more and more of the national budget. The steady expansion of the Great Society entitlements established during the Lyndon Johnson presidency exacerbated and politicized this conflict between civilian and military interests and funding. In the contest between "guns and butter," in times of peace democracies prefer "butter," a dynamic that can lead to military budgets being underfunded. But a permanent Cold War was a "twilight struggle," as John F. Kennedy called it in his inaugural speech, between peace and a war, one that sharpened the conflict between military and civilian fiscal priorities.

From this creation of a permanent military establishment, what the founding generation feared as a "standing army," followed a new dimension of the traditional wariness of the military—what General and President Dwight Eisenhower, in his 1961 Farewell Address

famously called the "military-industrial complex": that "conjunction of an immense military establishment and a large arms industry" whose "influence—economic, political, even spiritual—is felt in
every city, every statehouse, every office of the Federal government,"
encompassing "the very structure of our society. In the councils of
government, we must guard against the acquisition of unwarranted
influence, whether sought or unsought, by the military-industrial
complex. The potential for the disastrous rise of misplaced power
exists, and will persist."

One factor contributing to Eisenhower's warning is that our military and security establishment is housed in large federal agencies
concentrated in Washington, DC, close to Congress, which decides
their funding levels. Moreover, such large, hierarchically organized
bureaucracies, especially ones not accountable to the market or the
voters, are prone to professional deformation. The aims and interests
of the agency shift from the functions they were created to perform
to the interest of the agency itself. Institutional orthodoxy, received
wisdom, and unchallenged paradigms transform such agencies into
the proverbial "box" we're supposed to "think outside of." The les-
sons of history often cannot penetrate these silos of stale orthodoxy.

Such flaws, moreover, are worsened by the necessarily political nature of these bureaucracies. The heads of agencies like the
Department of Defense, housed in the Pentagon—the world's largest office building—are cabinet members appointed by the president
with the "advice and consent" of the Senate, and their rank and file
enjoy not just the protection of civil service laws but of a union as
well. Hence it is nearly impossible to fire them. And the proximity
to the Capitol and the White House, and the consulting, advocacy,
and lobbying firms clustered around both, leave these agencies open
to their influence.

These large agencies also negatively impact the military by offer-
ing the top military brass opportunities to serve in a president's cabinet. And, upon retirement, they can take lucrative seats on corporate
boards of armament manufacturers, or billets with lobbying firms,

where contacts from their years of service are useful in securing government contracts. The growth of cable news has also created opportunities to become regular contributors to news programs.

This bureaucratic dysfunction often interferes with the development of materiel adequate for our global responsibilities because of poor designs, exorbitant costs overruns, and serial missing of completion deadlines. Donald Devine of the *American Spectator* describes one of numerous examples of this problem:

> In the 1990s, joined by the Marines and Navy, they envisioned a Joint Strike Fighter, which ultimately led to today's Joint F-35 program. This took until 2015 to be fully operational after a first test flight a decade earlier. But it was very expensive at over $150 million per plane ($335 million counting development). Several variants were produced for U.S. and foreign services, with one abandoned after fewer than 200 copies, and another variant was forced to be an air-superiority fighter, "a role for which it is not suited [*Washington Post*]."[3]

Devine also mentions the air force's Boeing KC refueling tanker, just now entering service after twenty years but still not deemed "combat ready," and the navy's littoral ship for operations in shallower waters. First planned in the nineties, the first ship was launched in 2006. "Now," Devine writes, "15 years later, the Navy announced that it must retire nine of them, one of which was commissioned less than two years before, and the others had 'major propulsion issues.'"

All this is not to say that serving in such positions is necessarily about politics or greed, or that those who do so are not serving honorably. But this state of affairs is rife with moral hazard for both types of corruption, contributing to the disaffection with the military shared by many citizens. Finally, this long tradition of mistrust does not diminish the average citizen's admiration for those who serve the country in war; it's the powerful institutions and their perceived careerist or politicized leaders they don't trust, such as those high-ranking officers who pursue political aims like the "war on carbon" or critical race theory training curricula, rather than concentrating on our military preparedness and ability to defend the nation.

CONCLUSION

This survey of the "structures of democracy" provides the broader context for the topics included in this book's chapters. True to the founding ideals of the Hoover Institution's Role of Military History in Contemporary Conflict Working Group, the essays cover a variety of time periods and approach the topics of civilian and military conflict, war, and US foreign policy from a diversity of perspectives.

In chapter 1, Professor Paul Rahe documents one of the most famous examples of the excesses of ancient Athens' direct democracy, the trial and execution of six *stratēgoí*, elected officials who managed military affairs, after the victorious sea battle near Arginusae (406 BC). These officials were directly accountable to the citizens not just by elections but by indictments for actions that the citizens didn't like, with punishment including fines, exile, or execution. As the great orator of the fourth century BCE Demosthenes grouched of his compatriots' shortsighted refusal to vigorously check Philip of Macedon's adventurism, "So disgraceful is our condition now, that every general is put on trial two or three times before you for his life, though none dares even once to hazard his life against the enemy."[4] Excess accountability to the people, a danger the Founders tried to limit, can be as dangerous as too little.

Ralph Peters in chapter 2 analyzes the Civil War from the perspective of "dissent, resistance, and riot." His informative and lively written narrative reminds us that the divisive politics and civil violence we have witnessed, especially in the summer of 2020, is not that untypical in our history. Indeed, the levels of violence preceding and during the war, like the New York Draft Riot, were much higher and more lethal than anything experienced in subsequent American history. And contrary to the popular belief that North and South comprised unified blocks, there were dissenters in both regions, perhaps most famously the Copperheads, pro-Southern sympathizers in the North. The most heinous act of "dissent" came after the war with the Klan's terrorist insurgency against the occupying Union Army enforcing the new postwar settlement during Reconstruction.

In chapter 3, Professor Peter Mansoor writes a well-documented, important history of military dissent from the revolt of the admirals after World War II to the controversy over the incident in DC's Lafayette Square on June 1, 2020. This event sparked public pushback from the chair of the Joint Chiefs of Staff, Army General Mark Milley, who felt that he was duped into being a prop in President Trump's photo op. Mansoor argues that this public conflict between the president and the military's highest-ranking officer represents a new and dangerous deviation from the long tradition of uniformed dissent from the commander in chief, especially during the transition from one administration to the next.

Professor Williamson Murray's essay in chapter 4 covers the Cold War and the Korean War from the perspective of American isolationism, one of our oldest modes of dissent with regard to foreign relations and war. Murray provides a well-documented discussion of the conflict between George Kennan's strategy of containment and traditional isolationism. He describes how containment prevailed and gives us an analysis of the first major proxy duel of the Cold War, the Korean War, including its significant consequences both positive and negative

Chapter 5 comprises Bing West's study of dissent in the military and the objectives in war. Much of the internal dissent regards allocation of funds among the services, institutional organization, and disputes over tactics in the Vietnam and Korean Wars. Lost or inconclusive wars like Vietnam, Afghanistan, and Iraq produced more public dissent from the civilian government, especially the commander in chief and his cabinet; the perceptions and feelings of the citizen; and the officers and generals carrying out the policy. West provides a clearly written, detailed, economical narrative of each conflict and concludes with a discussion of the current conflict in Ukraine.

Finally, in his epilogue, Victor Davis Hanson, chair of the working group, provides a history of the mercurial and unconventional president Donald J. Trump's stormy relationships with his military cabinet members. The details of those years illustrate many of the tensions and dangers that have always characterized civilian–military relations and the principle of civilian control of the military. As Hanson concludes, "Between 2017 and 2022 we may have come close to violating these sacred boundaries, but then again these have been unusual times, in which the military–civilian system and the tradition of legitimate civilian dissent were tested as rarely before and survived—if perhaps only barely so."

All these essays are exemplary models of the purpose of the Hoover Institution's Role of Military History in Contemporary Conflict Working Group: keeping alive the importance of military history and its invaluable contribution to understanding our own times and challenges.

* * *

I personally am grateful for the professional acumen and patience of the Hoover Institution Press team: Barbara Arellano, Danica Michels Hodge, and John O'Rourke. I also thank my working group colleagues David Berkey and Megan R. Ring for their support.

NOTES

1. Winston Churchill, *The Second World War*, vol. I, *The Gathering Storm* (Boston: Houghton Mifflin, 1948; New York: Houghton Mifflin Harcourt, 1985), 16.

2. Thomas Sowell, *Intellectuals and Society* (New York: Basic Books, 2009), 183.

3. Donald Devine, "The Countless Failures of Big Bureaucracy," *American Spectator*, April 26, 2002.

4. Demosthenes, *First Philippic*, 47, trans. J. H. Vince (London: William Heinemann, 1930; Cambridge, MA: Harvard University Press, 2004).

1

CIVIL–MILITARY RELATIONS IN ANCIENT ATHENS: THE ARGINUSAE AFFAIR

Paul A. Rahe

Within the ancient Greek city, there was no distinction drawn between civilian and soldier. Every citizen was expected to serve, and serve they all did. But, as one would expect, those accorded a military command were in all the *póleis* held accountable by the ruling order. At Athens, which was a direct democracy, this meant that the instruments of popular governance—the probouleutic Council of 500, selected by lot from a large pool elected by the citizens in their ten tribes; the courts, which, with hundreds of jurors, were a microcosm of the city; and, on occasion, the assembly itself—sat in judgment over the *stratēgoí* placed in charge of the city's infantry, cavalry, and navy. During the Peloponnesian War, if not also before, the relationship between these bodies and the city's *stratēgoí* in the field was frequently poisonous—for the Athenians at home were wont to treat failure in the field not as a consequence of bad luck, poor preparation, or tactical incompetence but as a function of treason or bribery. The Arginusae trial is illustrative, and the details deserve careful attention.

THE CRISIS OF 406 BC

In the summer of 406 BC, before the battle of Arginusae was fought, the Athenians found themselves in desperate straits. Cyrus, the younger son of the Persian king Darius II, had arrived at Sardis the year before with gold aplenty, intent on funding a Lacedaemonian fleet that would secure their defeat. Moreover, at the request of the Spartan navarch Lysander son of Aristocritus, he had agreed to a measure that put the Athenians in a terrible bind—that the rowers in Sparta's fleet be paid four obols in silver a day rather than the three on offer from the Athenians.

Most of the rowers in the Athenian fleet were hirelings drawn from abroad, and Athens could not afford to match this wage. The city was virtually destitute. A great many of its allies were in rebellion; the tribute that funded its fleet was no longer coming in; and the Athenian *stratēgoí* were spending more time on quasi-piratical expeditions to raise money than on engaging the enemy.

It did not help that, while Athens's supreme commander Alcibiades son of Cleinias was absent on such an expedition, the man he had left in charge had acted in such a way as to occasion a brief battle in which the Athenians had lost something like a quarter of the fleet then quartered at Notium. It did not help that this spectacularly successful *stratēgós* was then cashiered and prudently withdrew into exile lest he be summoned into court and suffer execution. Nor did it help that his ablest lieutenants Thrasybulus son of Lycus and Theramenes son of Hagnon were also sidelined. For, although Conon son of Timotheos, the *stratēgós* placed in charge, was an able enough commander, he was not a tactical genius. So, when Lysander's successor Callicratidas launched a fleet far larger than the one that Conon, with the rowers who had not turned coat, was then able to deploy and when Conon set off to defend against the enemy armada as best he could the cities that Athens still controlled, the Athenian *stratēgós* not only suffered a defeat. He lost more than half of his galleys, and he found himself, with the remainder of Athens's expeditionary fleet, confined within Mytilene and the harbor to its south and subject to a siege. When word of Conon's plight reached home, his compatriots strove mightily to put together a relief expedition. If they did not succeed, they realized, the war would be over.[1]

Late in the summer of 407, when the Athenians had first learned of the Great King's decision to back the Lacedaemonians to the hilt and to dispatch his younger son to see to their victory, they had begun melting down golden dedications from their temples and minting gold coins to pay for a crash campaign to build new triremes.[2] It was this that enabled them to cobble together the fleet they dispatched thirty days after learning of Conon's predicament. These galleys they manned, as they had manned the fleet they had deployed at Salamis nearly three-quarters of a century before, by calling up everyone at Athens of an appropriate age—citizens, metics, and slaves— including the wealthy men who served in the cavalry. To the metics and the other foreigners who served, they offered citizenship. To the slaves who volunteered, they offered not only freedom but political rights of the sort that had been conferred on Athens's Plataean allies in 427 when their city was destroyed. This they had to do if they did not want this last class of rowers to desert to the Spartan side.[3] When, after pausing at Samos to pick up reinforcements, the Athenian *stratēgoí* departed for the coast of Lesbos, they had under their command a fleet of 150 ships manned by thirty thousand men.

THE BATTLE OF ARGINUSAE

As was the norm, there were ten men on the Athenian board of *stratēgoí* at this time. Conon was preoccupied at Mytilene, and his colleague Leon appears to have ended up in the custody of the Lacedaemonians. But Diomedon, Pericles son of Pericles, Aristocrates son of Scellias, Erasinides, Protomachus, Thrasyllus, Aristogenes, and Lysias were available; and every last one of them was dispatched with the Athenian fleet. It was this group of eight men that conducted the Athenian armada northward along the Anatolian coast from Samos. When they neared their goal, they stopped at the Arginusae isles, which lie just off the mainland of Asia Minor opposite Cape Malea, the southeasternmost point on the island of Lesbos.

At his behest, Callicratidas now had, we are told, 170 triremes. To keep Conon bottled up and to prevent the thirty-odd galleys still at his disposal from venturing forth and entering the fray, the Spartan navarch left fifty triremes at Mytilene under the command of a fellow Spartiate named Eteonicus. The remaining 120 he stationed down the Lesbian coast at Cape Malea.

The Athenian fleet was larger than its Spartan counterpart, and this was an advantage. But the force deployed by the Lacedaemonians was more fully combat-ready. It was manned by experienced mariners, and the crews of most of the individual ships had been operating together for some time. Moreover, many of these men had fought together at Notium, and nearly all the rest had experienced naval warfare in the fighting that had resulted in Conon's being trapped at Mytilene. By way of contrast, a high proportion of the Athenian crew members were landlubbers who had never seen service at sea. What these novices had going for them, however, was determination. They were—or soon would be—citizens of one sort or another; and for them, Athens's freedom and the advantages attendant on empire were at stake. They were not mercenaries like the men who rowed in Callicratidas's fleet. They were not inclined to prefer life and lucre to the liberty of their native land.

There are three Arginusae isles. One is a tiny speck that does not concern us here. The other two—called Garipasi and Kalemadasi—are fat fingers, parallel to one another, that stretch out from south to north just off the Anatolian coast. The Athenians camped on the former—which lay to the west of its twin. From there, when it was clear, they could see across the eight-mile-wide strait and be seen from the other side.

For a time, thanks to the Etesian winds that blow with some frequency from the north-northeast, the crews of these two fleets remained at rest, eyeing one another warily across the divide. In the middle of the night, when the wind tended to die down, Callicratidas made an attempt to put to sea in the hope that he might descend on the Athenians at the break of dawn and catch them flat-footed. But, we are told, heavy rain and thunder put a stop to this enterprise. It was not until the morning of the second day that the two fleets had at it.

Although the Athenian fleet was the larger of the two, it was operating at an even greater disadvantage than we have thus far noted. Many of the triremes deployed by Athens are apt to have been superannuated. Others were no doubt in poor repair, and a goodly number will not have been properly dried out in some time and will not have recently had their hulls scraped, recaulked, and recoated with pitch. Moreover, as we have seen, they sported ragtag crews unpracticed in what was a cooperative endeavor requiring considerable skill and close coordination. In consequence, these vessels were, for the most part, slow and awkward while the triremes facing them were quick and agile. The Athenians did not outclass their opponents, and they could not hope to outmaneuver them. To defeat the allied fleet, they had to outwit its navarch.

Thrasyllus, the most experienced of the Athenian *stratēgoí*, had had an undistinguished record as a commander. But he appears to have been a man who learned from experience. On this occasion, when at his urging, Athens's *stratēgoí* deployed their ships in line abreast, they did so in two lines—one behind the other. This well-known stratagem rendered it difficult, if not impossible, for the opposing helmsmen to resort to a row-through (*diékplous*)—whether it was their purpose to shear off the oars on the starboard or port side of an enemy trireme as they slipped through the enemy line; to perform thereafter an *anastrophḗ* and, after swinging around, strike such a galley in the hull or stern; or to attempt both in that order. Any ship that made its way through the first of the two lines of triremes would quickly find itself beset by the galleys in the second rank.

This decision eliminated one source of danger for the Athenians but at the price of giving rise to another no less serious. It meant that—if Callicratidas had his triremes deploy in line abreast in a single line, as any naval commander in his situation would be apt to do—his fleet would outflank that of the Athenians and be in a position to engulf it and to strike it from one or both flanks. Indeed, if circumstances were propitious, it might even be able to do so from behind.

To prevent this, the Athenian commanders, who were well versed in the principles of hoplite warfare, did something unprecedented. Their situation was dire. They knew that if the battle took place in the open sea, they would be defeated, that their fleet would in all likelihood be destroyed, and that they would lose the war, their empire, and, quite possibly, their city, their families, and their own lives. So, they refused to fight on unfavorable terms. According to Diodorus Siculus—who is almost certainly summarizing an account penned by the so-called Oxyrhynchus historian, an earlier analyst of real merit who was born at about the time of these events—they adopted a tactic familiar to every infantry general at the time, and they adapted it to the maritime situation in which they found themselves.

Their fleet, no doubt at Thrasyllus's urging, the Athenian *stratēgoí* divided into two units, and they held both back from the wide channel separating the Arginusae isles from Lesbos in such a way as to include Garipasi in their battle line. In consequence, the island and the peninsula that juts out from the mainland to its north covered both flanks of the Athenians' right wing while it afforded comparable protection to their left wing on its right. In principle, of course, Callicratidas could have dispatched a unit to circle around the islands from the south and come at the Athenians from behind, but the shallowness of the waters separating Garipasi from Kalemadasi and of those separating the latter from Anatolia to the east ruled this out.

The Athenian commanders' arrangement of their ships forced Callicratidas to divide his fleet in two—for otherwise his force would have been outflanked on one side or the other. But this configuration carried with it grave difficulties. It left the Spartan navarch with four flanks exposed—none of them in any way protected by a body of land. It is no wonder that his helmsman—a Megarian named Hermon—urged him to refuse battle, and he was a fool not to heed the advice offered by that old salt.[4]

Callicratidas could afford to wait, and time was on his side. But he was young, headstrong, and in a great hurry. What followed was, as Diodorus Siculus is quick to point out, the greatest sea battle hitherto known to the Greek world. Unfortunately, neither Xenophon of Athens, who is apt to have been present in a subordinate capacity with the Athenian fleet, nor Diodorus provides a full account. But what the two do have to say can for the most part be reconciled, and, on that basis, one can reconstruct what is likely to have happened.

Xenophon makes no mention of the Athenian commanders' deployment of their galleys on either side of Garipasi. But his description of their disposition of the vessels at their disposal is consistent with what we can glean from Diodorus's account. Between Garipasi and the mainland spur to its north, the span of water is restricted. To the south of this cigar-shaped island, there is open water. One would therefore expect that fewer triremes would be assigned to the Athenian right than to the Athenian fleet's other wing, and this is what Xenophon reports. The left and center Xenophon treats together, apparently as a single unit, and there he situates ninety triremes. The Athenian right he treats separately, as a distinct unit consisting of sixty triremes.

The two writers are also in agreement on one other matter—that Callicratidas commanded the Spartan right—and, given Diodorus's description of the configuration of the Athenian forces, that is where one would expect to find the Spartan commander. For the positioning of the Athenian galleys was favorable to there being little fighting in the north. The Athenian triremes there could not advance without making themselves vulnerable to an outflanking maneuver, the triremes in the opposing fleet were in no position to mount a frontal assault, and the Spartans and their allies in this unit could not turn their attention to the Athenian unit to the south of Garipasi without rendering themselves vulnerable to an attack from behind on the part of the Athenian unit to the island's north. The two contingents in the north were, in effect, locked in place—which is no doubt what the Athenian *stratēgoí* intended. It was in the south, where these commanders had stationed three-fifths of their fleet and where Callicratidas had situated himself, that the two fleets would be apt to clash.

The two writers are at odds on another matter, however. Xenophon reports that it was the Spartan left, in the north, that collapsed in the face of the Athenian onslaught while Diodorus reports that it was in the south, after a long struggle, that the Athenians won out and that, in the north, the Boeotians and the Euboeans held out until the victorious Athenians from the south turned on them and forced them to flee.

It is the latter narrative that makes sense. In the north, as we have seen, a stalemate was virtually inevitable—while, in the south, a clash was unavoidable. It is telling that Callicratidas was himself among those who lost their lives and that he reportedly did so when the trireme bearing him rammed an Athenian galley and he was either badly wounded in the melee that followed, as Diodorus reports, or hurled overboard at the moment of impact, as Xenophon claims. It is also telling that the Athenians destroyed or captured nine of the fleet's ten Laconian triremes, which surely accompanied the navarch. In the course of the day, Lacedaemon's allies lost another sixty to seventy triremes while the Athenians lost only twenty-five.[5]

Had a storm not blown up, the better part of what remained of the Athenian fleet would have descended on Mytilene and taken on the fifty triremes stationed there under the command of Eteonicus. As it happened, however, there was a storm, and it was exceedingly violent. In consequence, the Athenians had to take shelter once again on Garipasi.

In the meantime, Eteonicus, learning of Callicratidas's defeat, managed to prevent a panic by persuading his crews that Callicratidas had won. Then, no doubt as soon as the tempest began to abate and under the cover of night, he dispatched the fifty triremes under his command from Lesbos to Chios, where some of the triremes caught up in the battle had found refuge and where those that had fled and were driven by the storm to Aeolian Cumae and Phocaea eventually fetched up. Before returning to Chios himself, Eteonicus took

command of the hoplites stationed outside Mytilene and conducted
them overland on Lesbos either to Methymna, as Xenophon claims,
or to Pyrrha, as Diodorus reports. For their part, when the storm
passed and the Spartan fleet withdrew from Mytilene, Conon and
what remained of his fleet sallied forth to join the main Athenian
force, and the Athenians paid a fleeting visit to Chios and, having
accomplished nothing, withdrew to their stronghold on Samos.[6]

THE QUICK AND THE DEAD

In the aftermath of the battle at Arginusae, there was an attempt
on the part of the victors to recover the bodies of the dead, but it
had foundered. Moreover, they had not managed to pick up the
mariners who had survived the sinking of the twenty-five ships the
Athenians had lost, who had been unable to swim to shore, and who,
thereafter, were floating about in the water clinging to the flotsam
scattered across the strait separating Lesbos from the mainland. In
consequence, bloated bodies and the remains of triremes ended up
littering the coastline of the territory of Aeolian Cumae and Phocaea
ten to twenty-five miles to the south.[7]

It mattered little that the storm that had struck this strait soon
after the battle and that had prevented the fleet from proceeding
immediately to Mytilene had also rendered such a salvage operation impossible. An extraordinarily high proportion of those serving
in the emergency fleet had been citizens, and what seemed to the
unsuspecting glance to be an unnecessary loss of life and an impious
failure to bury the dead came to be deemed intolerable.

It is easy for us to understand the first of these concerns. No one
can be indifferent to the needless death of a loved one; and, thanks
in large part to the Sicilian expedition, the Athenians had by this
time experienced a nightmarish decade of needless deaths. To us,
however, the second concern may seem more of a puzzle. Burial is
not for us today as weighty a matter as it was for the ancient Greeks.
What we must recall to mind is the fact that the Hellenes were

persuaded that those left unburied would know no rest—that they would be condemned to wander the earth forever in distress. We must also give thought to the reasons why the chorus of Thebans in Sophocles's *Antigone* comes to be so sympathetic to the protagonist of that play. As Antigone insists, burial is first and foremost a family duty. In Athens, moreover, if Aelian can be trusted, it was also recognized as a civic duty. The written law of Athens reinforced the unwritten law of Hellas: it stipulated that a citizen who stumbled upon a corpse—even, apparently, the corpse of a foreigner—throw dirt upon it.[8]

The *stratēgoí* at Arginusae understood all of this. According to Diodorus, when these eight men rendezvoused at Garipasi after the battle to consider what to do next, they discussed not only rowing to Mytilene to destroy the Peloponnesian fleet besieging that city, to liberate Conon and the mariners with him, and to secure what was left of his fleet, but also recovering the Athenian dead. Xenophon confirms this report—although, where Diodorus refers solely to those killed, this Socratic rationalist tellingly mentions only those still alive. To this, the latter adds that the *stratēgoí* resolved to divide the fleet and accomplish both tasks: the fleet's commanders were to make their way to Mytilene with most of the remaining triremes while Alcibiades's erstwhile associates Theramenes and Thrasybulus and some of the taxiarchs set out with forty-six galleys to rescue the shipwrecked. Diodorus reports that both parties actually set out, that the crews on the ships assigned to pick up the corpses began to raise fierce objections when a storm came up and the sea became dangerously choppy, and that, when the storm grew more violent, both parties fled back to Garipasi. That the tempest rendered salvage impossible Xenophon agrees.[9]

If Xenophon's account of a speech that Alcibiades's kinsman Euryptolemos son of Peisanax subsequently delivered before the Athenian assembly can be trusted, when the *stratēgoí* first met after the battle, Diomedon suggested that they devote their resources to picking up the shipwrecked men, Erasinides urged that they head for Mytilene, and Thrasyllus proposed the measure agreed upon—that they divide the fleet and do both. Euryptolemos also reports that the *stratēgoí* met once again after the storm.

By that time, it was too late to save the lives of the shipwrecked. Moreover, thanks to the storm, the bodies of the dead were carried a considerable distance to the south and scattered so far and wide that they were, for all practical purposes, unrecoverable. So, instead of pondering what to do, the *stratēgoí* discussed how they were to explain what they had not done—which, back home, might well be regarded as negligence and a dereliction of duty. It was Euryptolemos's claim that his friend Diomedon and his kinsman Pericles talked their colleagues out of dispatching a report to the Council of 500 and the assembly back home blaming the failure to mount an effective salvage operation on Theramenes, Thrasybulus, and the taxiarchs; and it is clear that no such allegations were included in the official report the eight dispatched and that in it they contended that the storm rendered it impossible for anyone to do anything.[10]

THE ARGINUSAE TRIAL

Xenophon also tells us that, not long after the battle, the eight *stratēgoí* participants in it were relieved of duty and that, as a stopgap, Adeimantus and Philocles were sent to Samos to fill in for them and share the command with Conon. The Athenian historian also implies what Diodorus tells us explicitly: that these eight men were recalled to Athens. Two in their number—Protomachus and Aristogenes—ruminated on the character of their compatriots, calculated the danger that they were apt to face, and opted to ignore the summons, knowing full well that, as a consequence, they would be exiled, their property would be confiscated, and they would be condemned to death. The other six—Pericles, Diomedon, Erasinides, Lysias, Aristocrates, and Thrasyllus—had more confidence in their compatriots and made their way home as required—where, without ever being given a proper hearing, they were condemned and executed.[11]

The details need not detain us for long. It should suffice to say that—had the *stratēgoí* blamed on Theramenes, Thrasybulus, and the taxiarchs the failure to recover the survivors and the bodies of the dead, as some of them were inclined to do—they might have saved their own skins at the expense of the lives of others who were no less innocent. In the event, wrongly suspecting that Theramenes and Thrasybulus, who had returned to Athens soon after the battle, were behind their deposition, some in their number wrote letters imputing responsibility to those two trierarchs and their colleagues. In the assembly, Theramenes responded by drawing attention to the fact that, in their official dispatch, the *stratēgoí* had mentioned nothing of the kind. In consequence, the dispatch of these letters looked like an awkward attempt at evading responsibility, and the implication of their dodge was that someone really had engaged in gross misconduct.

None of this much mattered. What mattered most is that the eight generals at Arginusae had pulled off a near miracle, that the war with Lacedaemon was by no means over, that new triremes would be built to replace those that the Spartans had lost, and that—with Alcibiades in exile and Thrasybulus and Theramenes in effect barred from high office—Athens was desperately short of military talent. It also mattered that the six *stratēgoí* who had returned home were never given a full opportunity to defend their conduct. Instead, in the wake of a festival focused on the family that occasioned a great outpouring of grief on the part of those who had lost loved ones, a shadowy figure named Callixeinos persuaded the Council of 500 to propose to the assembly a *proboúleuma* providing that the fate of all six commanders be decided forthwith by a vote in that assembly, that intimidation was brought to bear on those who insisted that such a procedure was contrary to Athenian law and tried to block its implementation by way of a legal maneuver, that the *proboúleuma* was adopted, and that the *stratēgoí* were condemned and killed.[12]

Never before in human history and, as far as we know, never thereafter did a self-governing people inflict damage on themselves on a scale comparable to this. First, the Athenians deprived themselves of the service of the ablest of their commanders, Alcibiades. Then, they relegated to a secondary role his exceptionally capable associates Thrasybulus and Theramenes. And, finally, they executed or drove into exile the men of less renown who proved able, at a moment of supreme danger, to fill the shoes of these three men. With all the advantages that they possessed in the wake of Athens's Sicilian catastrophe, the Lacedaemonians were not able to defeat Athens . . . until the Athenians voted for suicide. As the easy Spartan victory at Aegospotami made clear, the *stratēgoí* who took office in the spring of 405 were not up to the challenge Athens then faced.

The Arginusae affair was a shocking event; and it was, strictly speaking, unprecedented. But to call it an aberration would be to go too far. The Athenians were not in the habit of punishing successful *stratēgoí*, but, as I have already observed, they did tend to treat failure in the field as a crime, and in such cases capital punishment could be imposed and sometimes was. With some frequency, moreover, the Athenians levied swinging fines on commanders who suffered defeat; and Protomachus and Aristogenes were by no means the first *stratēgoí* who, when cashiered, withdrew into exile for fear of suffering something much worse than a fine if they returned home. Moreover, this pattern of conduct on the part of the Council of 500, the courts, and the assembly at Athens influenced the calculations of the city's commanders in a fashion apt to damage the city.

Athens's venture in Sicily is a case in point. It was a high-risk operation from the outset. Had Nicias son of Niceratus chosen to withdraw late in the summer of 414 when things began to go badly wrong, the Athenian losses would have been modest. Had Nicias, Demosthenes son of Alcisthenes, and Eurymedon son of Eucles been willing to do so in 413 when they had exhausted all their offensive options, the losses would have been less modest but not devastating. In the event, however, for fear of what they would suffer at the hands of their compatriots if they returned home in defeat, these *stratēgoí* took risks that they knew to be foolhardy and, in the process, turned what would have been a humiliating loss into a catastrophe sufficient to occasion the Spartan-Persian alliance and the rebellion of a great many of Athens's subject allies. At Athens, civil–military relations, in the restricted sense considered here, were quite literally toxic. The Arginusae affair was the icing on a poisonous cake long in the making, and the *stratēgoí* executed in 406 were by no means the only Athenians made to die as a consequence of its consumption.[13]

NOTES

1. See Xenophon, *Hellenica* 1.5.1–6.24; Diodorus 13.70.1–74.4, 76.2–79.7; and Plutarch, *Alcibiades* 35.1–36.5 with Donald Kagan, *The Fall of the Athenian Empire* (Ithaca, NY: Cornell University Press, 1987), 293–337. In referring to the fragments surviving from the lost works of the ancient Greek historians, I cite *Die Fragmente der Griechischen Historiker*, ed. Felix Jacoby (Leiden: E. J. Brill, 1993) as *FGrH* by the number assigned the historian and the number assigned the fragment.

2. In 407/6, the Athenians melted down golden dedications from their temples to pay for a crash campaign to produce triremes: Scholia Aristophanes *Frogs* 720 = Hellanicus *FGrH* 323a F25 with Wesley E. Thompson, "The Golden Nikai and the Coinage of Athens," *Numismatic Chronicle*, seventh series, 10 (1970): 1–6, read in light of *Inscriptiones Graecae* I³ 117 = *Greek Historical Inscriptions, 478–404 BC*, ed. Robin Osborne and P. J. Rhodes (Oxford: Oxford University Press, 2017), no. 188.

3. Athenians ready fleet, slave and free, even *hippeîs* called up to serve: Xenophon, *Hellenica* 1.6.24. Freedom and political rights on the Plataean model offered and eventually awarded the slaves who participated: consider Aristophanes. *Frogs* 33, 190–91, 693–94, 693–702 with the scholia (especially the one for 693–94 that cites Hellanicus *FGrH* 323a F25) in light of Thucydides 3.68.103 and Demosthenes 59.104. See also Peter Hunt, "The Slaves and the Generals of Arginusae," *American Journal of Philology* 122, no. 3 (Autumn 2001): 359–80 (esp. 359–70).

4. Arrangement of the battle lines at Arginusae: Xenophon, *Hellenica* 1.6.29–32 and Diodorus, 13.98, which should be read in light of Sosylus *FGrH* 176 F1. Indication that Thrasyllus was the dominant Athenian *stratēgós* on the board: Lysias 21.7. Note Graham Wylie, "The Battle of the Arginusae: A Reappraisal," *Civiltà Classica e Cristiana* 11 (1990): 234–49, and see Godfrey Hutchinson, *Attrition: Aspects of Command in the Peloponnesian War* (Stonehouse, Gloucestershire: Spellmount, 2006), 198–202, and Debra Hamel, *The Battle of Arginusae: Victory at Sea and Its Tragic Aftermath in the Final Years of the Peloponnesian War* (Baltimore: Johns Hopkins University Press, 2015), 45–50.

Hamel provides a compelling defense of the Sicilian historian's account and Hutchinson and Hamel supply a persuasive analysis of the disposition of the galleys on the two sides. Regarding the papyrus fragments of the Oxyrhynchus historian found in Egypt and the evidence that, in dealing with this period, Diodorus or his source is epitomizing his narrative, see I. A. F. Bruce, introduction to *An Historical Commentary on the Hellenica Oxyrhynchia* (Cambridge: Cambridge University Press, 1967), 1–27, and Richard Billows, "The Authorship of the *Hellenica Oxyrhynchia*," *Mouseion*, third series, 9, no. 3 (2009): 219–38. Billows makes, in my opinion, a persuasive case that this author was Thucydides's great admirer Theopompus of Chios.

5. Battle of Arginusae: consider Diodorus 13.98.5–99.5, 100.1, 3, in conjunction with Xenophon, *Hellenica* 1.6.33–34, and see Wylie, "The Battle at the Arginusae," 241–43, who asks all the right questions, and Hamel, *The Battle of Arginusae*, 50–53, who best answers them. Diodorus errs in only one particular: he situates the Athenian *stratēgós* Pericles on the Athenian right in the north with Thrasyllus, then has Callicratidas, who was stationed, as both Xenophon and Diodorus agree, on the Spartan right in the south, ram his trireme: Diodorus 13.98.3, 99.3–4. Xenophon is probably correct in situating Pericles on the Athenian left in the south: *Hellenica* 1.6.29.

6. Post-battle storm, the escape of Eteonicus's fleet and the retreat of his hoplites; Conon joins the main Athenian force: Xenophon, *Hellenica* 1.6.35–38 and Diodorus 13.100.5–6 with Kagan, *The Fall of the Athenian Empire*, 352–53. Eteonicus resurfaces on Chios: Xenophon, *Hellenica* 2.1.1.

7. Failure to recover the quick and the dead after Arginusae: Xenophon, *Hellenica* 1.7.34–35, Diodorus, 13.100.1–4.

8. The fate of the unburied dead: Homer, *Iliad* 23.71–74, *Odyssey* 11.55–83; Euripides, *Hecuba* 27–34, *Trojan Women* 1081–85. Burial a family duty: Sophocles, *Antigone* 77, 450–55, 745, 749. Athenian law: Aelian *Varia Historia* 5.14. For further evidence and a citation of the extensive secondary literature on this question, see Alexander Rubel, *Fear and Loathing in Ancient Athens: Religion and Politics during the Peloponnesian War*, trans. Michael Vickers and Alina Piftor (Durham, UK: Acumen Publishing, 2014), 137–41.

9. Post-battle deliberations of the *stratēgoí* at Garipasi: Xenophon, *Hellenica* 1.6.35 and Diodorus 13.100 with Martin Ostwald, *From Popular Sovereignty to the Sovereignty of Law: Law, Society, and Politics in Fifth-Century Athens* (Berkeley: University of California Press, 1986), 434, and Kagan, *The Fall of the Athenian Empire*, 354–62.

10. Claims attributed to Euryptolemos: Xenophon, *Hellenica* 1.7.16–18, 29–31. Generals' report blames the storm: 1.7.4–6. See Kagan, *The Fall of the Athenian Empire*, 362–63.

11. Arginusae *stratēgoí* deposed and recalled, six return: Xenophon, *Hellenica* 1.7.1–2 with Diodorus 13.101.1–5 with Ostwald, *From Popular Sovereignty to the Sovereignty of Law*, 434–35.

12. The Arginusae trial: Xenophon, *Hellenica* 1.7 and Diodorus 13.101.1–103.2 with Antony Andrewes, "The Arginousai Trial," *Phoenix* 28, no. 2 (Spring 1974): 112–22; Ostwald, *From Popular Sovereignty to the Sovereignty of Law*, 436–45; and Kagan, *The Fall of the Athenian Empire*, 363–75. For an intelligent, if at times highly speculative, reconstruction of events, see Hamel, *The Battle of Arginusae*, 71–89. The charges that Xenophon lodges against Theramenes are hard to believe given Lysias's silence in this regard in his denunciation of the man: 12.62–78.

13. For the evidence pertaining to the penalties inflicted on Athens's *stratēgoí* in this period, see Debra Hamel, *Athenian Generals: Military Authority in the Classical Period* (Leiden: Brill, 1998), 141–46. For the cases where the evidence is dispositive: see nos. 8–9, 12–16, 20–21. For cases where the evidence is merely suggestive, see nos. 5–7, 10–11, 17. For evidence suggesting that a general was deposed, see nos. 18–19 and perhaps 22. For an overview, see Hamel, *The Battle of Arginusae*, 59–70. Thanks to the democratic predilections increasingly prevalent in the last two centuries, there is a substantial secondary literature devoted to defending what I regard as indefensible—Athens's treatment of its *stratēgoí*. For a recent example, where much of the earlier literature of this sort is cited, see Dustin Gish, "Defending *Dēmokratia*: Athenian Justice and the Trial of the Arginusae Generals," in *Xenophon: Ethical Principles and Historical Enquiry*, ed. Fiona Hobden and Christopher Tuplin (Leiden: Brill, 2012), 161–212. For a more sensible assessment, see Fred S. Naiden, "The Crime of Defeat," in *Kállistos Nómos: Scritti in onore di Alberto Maffi*, ed. Barbara Biscotti (Turin: Giappichella, 2018), 103–19.

2

DISSENT, RESISTANCE, AND RIOT IN THE AMERICAN CIVIL WAR

Ralph Peters

Ill-taught and unabsorbed, romanticized, demonized, and fiercely politicized, the history of the United States remains stubbornly inspirational, powerfully instructive, and, ultimately, comforting for those willing to study it before drawing their conclusions. Bruised but incorruptible, that battered spouse among the Muses, Clio, clings stalwartly to facts in the face of all the abuse the intellectually corrupt and ethically untethered bring to bear against her. And the facts of our history tell us that, for all the bad behavior, ingratitude, and chicanery of the moment, the past was worse and we somehow made the best of it.

If our day seems vivid with peril, it is because we have taken so much for granted; if the menace of the moment appears unprecedented, it is because we refuse to recognize the tumult and disarray that preceded our challenges. To borrow a German saying, *Die Lage war immer so ernst*, which we may translate loosely as "The sky has always been falling." Indeed, a century and a half ago, the collapsing heavens seemed about to crush us.

Let us then begin this consideration of dissent, resistance, and riot in the American Civil War with a pair of grim numbers that, paradoxically, might reassure us: our civil war took the lives of at least 740,000 Americans. Were today's United States to suffer proportionate violence, 7,700,000 of us would die. But we shall not suffer that violence: the orgy of ignorance and spite we witnessed on

January 6, 2021, was a national embarrassment, not a second Fort
Sumter.

We've had it much worse. The heyday of American political violence, riot, and assassination was not the reeling 1960s or the ornery
past few years, but the near century between the 1820s and 1900,
with nation-rending violence concentrated between the establishment of Kansas as a territory in 1854—which lit the ready fuse of
civil war—and the disputed election of 1876, which reduced the
Union military victory to a political draw whose consequences echo
to this day.

The sky *has* always been falling.

BY THE NUMBERS

To reach beyond apparent similarities to the profound differences
between that reverberant past and our own spell of spite and disori-
entation, a few statistics help. In 1860, on the eve of civil war, the population of the United States was 31.5 million. That number reflected
a 40 percent increase over barely a decade, as European disasters and
upheavals flooded our land with immigrants. The equivalent today
would be 130 million newcomers arriving in a single decade: the dis-
ruption such an inflow would provoke is all but unimaginable.

Yet, immigration did not spark our civil war (although it produced
plenty of local violence—see below). What immigration did was to
facilitate the Union military victory by providing the burgeoning
North with immense reserves of manpower, while the less welcom-
ing and less prosperous South struggled bitterly to refill dwindling
ranks. Indeed, the lopsided population distribution would have
warned anyone other than the South's self-deluding firebrands from
taking up arms in secession: the states that would remain within the
Union had 23 million inhabitants, native-born or newly arrived. The
South claimed nine million, four million of whom were slaves (dis-
tributed among a mere three thousand slaveholders; this was, indeed,
a rich man's war and a poor man's fight).

The North was increasingly urban and industrialized—powering into modernity—while the South remained largely rural and agricultural. Only three Southern cities ranked amid the top twenty-five in population, with New Orleans the largest at number six, its population 168,000. No other Southern city came close: Richmond, destined to be the capital of the Confederacy, sneaked in at the twenty-fifth position with thirty-eight thousand residents. New York City and Brooklyn (separate entities then) presented a combined population of over a million—equivalent to fully 20 percent of the entire White population of the Confederacy. Philadelphia alone held over half a million citizens and new arrivals.

While the four million human beings held in bondage in the South provided a catalyst for war (and today's activist "historians" ignore that the United States is the only country in history that fought a civil war over slavery, suffering one war death for every five slaves freed), the differences between North and South went even deeper, reflecting an Atlantic world in uproar as traditional societies struggled to cope with the velocity of change: our civil war was, among other things, a bloody argument over national identity, social structures, economics, labor, the distribution of political authority, and even literacy (in a practical sense, the Union won the war with forms filled out in triplicate—notably higher literacy rates in the Northern states enabled the swift establishment of a modern military bureaucracy; it's only a slight exaggeration to say that the South lost because it couldn't spell: a valiant-but-illiterate soldier might make a fine infantryman, but he wouldn't do as a company first sergeant).

This was a contest between cultures—our original culture war—a rear-guard action waged vainly by feudal remnants against an inevitable, destabilizing future.

Q-ANON 1861

We, the People, did not need to wait for the internet to embrace, amplify, and weaponize disinformation. In mid-nineteenth-century

America, the media of the day behaved even less responsibly and
with less regard for veracity than extremist websites do today.
Conspiracy theories were rampant and, while contemporary hyster-
ics lead to acrimony at school-board meetings, the fantastic claims of
newspapers in the 1850s pushed our country toward civil war.

Convinced that we are unique in our trials, we insist that the collapse of objective reality on the internet is an unprecedented phenomenon. It is not. The allure of "secret" explanations that excuse
our failures and assign blame for our misfortunes appears to be as
old as humanity, but it certainly expanded with the first information revolution, the development of alphabets and narrative writing.
Then the second information revolution, ignited by the development of reusable type for the printing press in mid-fifteenth-century
Mainz, unleashed a flood of information and disinformation that
rendered "knowledge" uncontrollable by central authorities, trigger-
ing, among other shocks, the Protestant Reformation, which speed-
ily shattered the data-control and data-analysis mechanism that had
prevailed in Europe for almost twelve centuries, since the Battle of
the Milvian Bridge; a transgressive flood of claims and counterclaims
quickly triggered 130 years of the most brutal warfare and repression
on European soil prior to the twentieth century.

That second information revolution never ended: there's been
an uninterrupted expansion of information flow from Gutenberg
to Google; however, an important stage in that ongoing revolution
began in the eighteenth century with the appearance of popular
news sheets. By the mid-nineteenth century, lowered printing costs,
expanding literacy, and increased wealth had spawned thousands of
multipage newspapers in Europe and the Americas—far more than
exist today—and competition was fierce. In the United States, every
town seemed to boast at least one newspaper and, often, two or more
to reflect party politics. As ever, sensation sold. Before the formal age
of tabloid journalism everything seemed to be tabloid journalism,
with breathtaking accusations, grotesque insults, ethnic and religious
partisanship, and plain meanness all in a day's expenditure of ink.
Madcap libels abounded, making today's excesses seem almost prim.

As the nation blundered and blustered toward division, nothing sold better than warning of the monstrosities that would come in the wake of abolition. The term "miscegenation" had not yet come into vogue and the prevailing watchword was "amalgamation," as pro-slavery editors (not least, in border states or northern cities) warned laborers and clerks, merchants and farmhands, that once the abolitionists had freed the slaves, they intended to force White women to breed with Black males. The organizational mechanisms of such a program were never explained and did not have to be: pro-Southern journalists had found a topic that could be endlessly reprised and that excited profound dread (we may debate whether such fears are atavistic or learned, missing the essential point that they're reliable).

The second accusation commonly leveled against the abolitionists was that freed Blacks would be brought north as cheap laborers, putting workmen—particularly new and unskilled immigrants—out of their jobs. This claim had particular force among the masses of recent Irish immigrants, most of whom were employed in menial and already-tenuous work.

In a fracturing nation tormented by the issue of the extension of slavery into the western territories, the racial hatred inflamed by a metastasizing, irresponsible media makes today's social tensions appear almost benign.

And if hatred was good for the newspaper business, war was wonderful.

PRAIRIE ATROCITIES

Violence began in earnest in the Kansas Territory, seven years before an aging fanatic yanked a lanyard in Charleston. The federal government had decreed that the local population would vote to decide whether Kansas would be a slave state or a "free soil" state (the same rule applied to the neighboring Nebraska Territory, but slavery was never an issue there). Southern sympathizers grasped the initiative, drafting a pro-slavery state constitution and holding a vote that was, indeed, a "big steal," as hundreds of Missourians crossed into the thinly populated territory to cast pro-slavery votes (some towns recorded twice as many votes as they had registered voters). The pro-Southern Pierce administration recognized the results (the subsequent Buchanan administration would also tilt pro-slavery), provoking outrage among sodbuster settlers from the North. Soon, the local issue would engage the nation and attract fanatics and terrorists from both camps.

Perhaps the surest measure of the westward shift of the frontier came as the number of settlers murdered by White men exceeded the tally of those killed by Indians. Southern sympathizers were quicker—indeed, eager—to kill, but the Free Soilers, soon to be known also as "Jayhawkers," began to organize in turn. Individual corpses gave way to the spectacle of small massacres. A destructive raid on the free-soil town of Lawrence prefigured large-scale butchery that would follow in the war years.

Then a catalytic figure appeared. As fanatical a would-be messiah as this country ever produced, John Brown pursued his own holy war. If his cause appears righteous today, his methods were appalling. He engaged in genuine terror, murdering men not on proof of transgressions but over the mere suspicion of unwanted sympathies. A celebrity among intellectuals, Brown delivered a seductive frisson to New England abolitionists, much as Che Guevara would do for their great-great-grandchildren. Brown gave them corpses and they gave him money for arms. As ever, the intelligentsia could applaud its own self-righteousness while avoiding personal risk.

Brown's life would end on the gallows before the formal war began, but he remains a controversial—and decidedly compelling—figure today. But if Brown passed into history, his opposite numbers on the prairie would pass into legend.

As power shifted from a disintegrating pro-slavery territorial government to a free-soil majority, Southern-sympathizing guerrillas, "border ruffians," grew ever more brutal. Both sides committed atrocities and would commit far graver ones during the war, and the small-scale combat in Kansas and western Missouri came to display a routine savagery, a sadistic cruelty, seen nowhere else in the course of the conflict; elsewhere, from Fort Pillow to the Petersburg Crater, wanton brutality might erupt, but only on the frontier was it the norm.

When Kansas at last entered the Union as a free state on the eve of the war, the pro-Southern guerrillas avoided incorporation into regular Confederate forces to wage an autonomous insurgency against federal authority. Charismatic, blood-soaked leaders emerged, such as William Quantrill and "Bloody Bill" Anderson, raiding, burning, and slaughtering, their appetite for violence insatiable. On August 21, 1863, guerrilla forces combined for a mass attack on Lawrence, in the course of which at least 130 (and probably dozens more) males were executed. The victims were not soldiers but barbers and livery-stable hands, barkeeps and laborers, husbands, fathers, and sons whose sole guilt lay in making their homes in a town held sympathetic to the Union. It was, arguably, the worst planned atrocity in American history.

Then, on September 27, 1864, in the desperate, lawless days of a failing war, pro-slavery irregulars ambushed a Union military column near Centralia, Missouri. The Union dead numbered 125 officers and men, many tortured to death after surrendering and found scalped, with ears and genitals cut off. Their corpses were left to rot in a spectacle worthy of today's confessional terrorists.

Quantrill and Anderson both died before the war's end, but, for years thereafter, their understudies continued an itinerant insurrection sustained by banditry . . . Frank and Jesse James, Cole Younger . . . cold-blooded killers who would become Hollywood heroes long after their deaths.

APPALACHIAN YANKEES, DISSENTING FROM THE DISSENTERS

A classic example of history reversed in the popular consciousness is a Confederate battle flag displayed on a pickup truck in West Virginia—or almost anywhere else in the high Appalachians. During the Civil War, this was Union country, the "land of no cotton," yet today, residents assume that their ancestors must have worn gray or butternut while worshiping Robert E. Lee. Dissecting this metamorphosis is beyond the reach of this essay, yet the phenomenon illustrates the malleability of transmitted memory.

Forgetting, too, is part of the shaping and reshaping of history to answer current interests. When addressing Abraham Lincoln's commitment to preserving the Union and not allowing the Confederacy to go its own way (had they managed to sustain secession, Confederate states would soon enough have been seceding from the Confederacy—most had only slavery in common and local allegiances were paramount), today's historians often overlook the stubborn allegiance to the Union of mountain folk from western Maryland to northern Alabama. To accept the Confederate secession would have meant abandoning a significant number of loyal Americans.

The formula behind this Appalachian adhesion to the Union was straightforward: cotton, the product that tyrannized the Southern states, is a lowland crop. And cotton culture depended on slavery to remain economically viable. Throughout the South, the higher the elevation, the fewer the slaves: the hardscrabble Scots-Irish farmers working windswept fields rarely encountered Black faces on their nobs or in their hollows—unless those passersby belonged to backcountry communities of runaway slaves and renegade Whites (among whom the dreaded "amalgamation" proved voluntary). Mountain culture was profoundly separate from the feudal structures of the plantation lowlands.

Beyond the well-known separation of western Virginia from the rest of the state, contests for loyalties and local conflicts abounded. Thanks not least to the population of its eastern highlands, Kentucky remained in the Union, while a desperate Confederate move into eastern Tennessee proved to be more of an occupation than a liberation; likewise, Southern attempts to recruit in western Maryland repeatedly met frustration. In general, border states provided regiments to both sides; yet, as the war progressed the federals were able to recruit a cavalry regiment from Union sympathizers as far south as Alabama (the all-white 1st Alabama Cavalry, plus four infantry regiments composed of former slaves), but there was never going to be a 1st Pennsylvania Infantry in service to the Confederacy.

There were few significant battles in the high mountains, whose terrain and climate were inhospitable to large-scale maneuvers, but there were plenty of skirmishes and small-unit actions (future president Rutherford B. Hayes built up his calf muscles leading an Ohio regiment up and down the mountains of western Virginia). There were also plenty of local feuds and killings in a war that often divided families or set clans in opposition to one another: the war brought opportunities to settle personal scores. Nonetheless, the violence never approached the atrocious levels seen in Kansas and western Missouri. Killing was apt to happen as a result of bushwhacking, not in an organized attempt to seize towns or depopulate terrain, and many of the ugliest—if still small-scale—incidents occurred late in the war, as Confederate armies suffered gutting attrition and sought to force mountain residents into their ranks through a vengeful draft. Nor did the wartime hatreds disappear with the collapse of the Confederacy: local grudges lingered for decades and longer.

And yet . . . and yet . . . today the great-great-great-grandson of the highlander killed in an up-the-holler fight with a gray-coated press-gang flies a Confederate flag on his front porch.

THE GREATEST CITY SUNDERED

The eruption of murderous violence, arson, and plunder that wracked New York City for four days, from July 13 through 16, 1863, remains the deadliest and most destructive riot of any kind on United States soil. It was a race riot. It was a class riot. And it was an antidraft riot. Desperate to minimize the horror, the nascent Tammany Hall political machine (soon to be notorious in its own right) put the official death count at 105. Responsible historians count at least 500 dead. Still other calculations put the body count between 1,000 and over

2,000. The precise number was not known by anyone in 1863 and cannot be known now, but the magnitude of the death and destruction (the latter estimated to have been at least forty million dollars) mortified all parties—and even were we to accept the preposterously low official casualty estimate, the New York Draft Riot would remain the bloodiest American violence that did not take place on a battlefield.

Of note, New York had been, literally, a riotous city for decades, with bursts of destructive violence over everything from politics to immigration, from speeches to music-hall programs, but the Draft Riot remains unique.

The trigger was the (already once-postponed) draft lottery. As the supply of ready volunteers for the Union armies neared exhaustion, the Lincoln administration saw a draft as essential, if unwelcome. The impact on New York City's population was primed to become particularly telling, due to previous Democrat Party machinations: for over a decade, politicians had granted Irish immigrants instant citizenship by adding them to the voting rolls as quickly as registry pens could be dipped in ink. Those voting lists now served to identify potential draftees—something for which few immigrants felt enthusiasm.

The Irish position in American society in mid-1863 was complex. Settled Irish citizens had developed loyalty to the Union, and, early in the war, Irish volunteers had proved plentiful and spectacularly courageous. Recent immigrants, however, were usually at the bottom of the societal ladder (which, in their case, was missing several rungs), meanly employed or jobless and living in squalid, crowded conditions hardly conducive to inspiring patriotism.

To rub in the inequities felt by the "new" Irish, the draft law allowed upper-middle-class and wealthy males to buy their way out of military service by paying $300 to provide a substitute (the mechanics of this loophole were messy and corrupt, as well). In a city of grim contrasts—far graver and deeper than urban disparities today—the rich had already excited sufficient resentment . . . and letting well-tailored gentlemen buy their way out of the war proved a last straw (a substantial number of wealthy young men had already evaded service by establishing themselves in Europe for the duration, although others of high fortune volunteered and gave their lives).

Beyond these issues, race loomed, and demagogues warned unskilled immigrants that even the humblest jobs would soon be reserved for freed Blacks who would do the work still more cheaply. Given that established Black freemen frequently had prospered and had built thriving neighborhoods, racial jealousy long had been simmering, as angry Whites found Black "wealth" insulting and provocative.

Thus, on the thirteenth of July, ten days after the climax of the Battle of Gettysburg, the just-begun draft lottery, class resentments, and racial tension combined to draw first blood—egged on by the media of the day and, in particular, by the exuberantly unscrupulous Manton Marble, editor of the *New York World*, who might well serve as the patron saint of the most extreme and irresponsible media figures of our own day. (On the other hand, the cantankerous Horace Greeley, whose *New-York Tribune* was viewed as sympathetic to abolition, became a prime target of a lynch mob; yet he reported to his office every day during the rioting, even as his employees took up arms to defend themselves.)

New York City authorities were utterly unprepared for the scale of the rioting that swept rapidly through immigrant neighborhoods (of note, however, some of the grimmest slums, such as Five Points, did not participate in the riot—in Marxist terms, this was a protest of the emerging proletariat, not of the parasitic *Lumpenproletariat*). Meanwhile, the military forces normally on hand, including the New York Militia, had been dispatched to support the Gettysburg campaign (which they failed to join in time). The senior military figure present, Major General John E. Wool, was well past his prime, indecisive, and, at the moment, in command of little more than a squad of quarreling staff officers. Civilian leadership froze. There were no clear lines of authority and everyone squabbled over who was responsible for each new catastrophe. From the start, the Metropolitan Police Department performed heroically, striving to calm the swelling crowds until the police commissioner had been beaten unconscious and police lines overrun—at which point fire-arms came into play. As did looted alcohol.

Contrary to a belief held at the time, the rioting had not been pro-voked by Confederate agents. The participants did not act according to a plan. Their initial targets were whatever and whoever appeared at hand, but Black Manhattanites, visually obvious and comparatively well dressed, were among the first—and last—victims. Black busi-nesses and homes were looted and burned. Family men were beaten to death still ignorant of the general upheaval. In a particularly hate-ful act, one of the many sub-mobs burned down the Colored Orphan Asylum, whose inmates had been rescued due only to the courage of outnumbered authorities on the scene.

The response of the citizenry varied. Approximately forty thou-sand New Yorkers are believed to have joined the mobs, but over 90 percent of the population did not, including many of the Irish. Some Irish families protected and harbored Black neighbors. The Irish-heavy police force remained loyal and largely disciplined. Nor were the rioters exclusively Irish but included recently arrived German and other immigrants, as well as the native-born louts and trouble-seekers who join mobs everywhere.

As more opportunists entered the ranks of the rioters, targets expanded to arsenals, government institutions, Protestant churches, shops, and hotels. The military scrambled to assemble troops, call-ing in tiny army and marine garrisons from the harbor forts and beseeching Albany and Washington for artillery—which ultimately would fire down New York City avenues before the riot was quelled. Additional forces rushed back to the city and violence persisted, as rioters refused to dissolve even as the soldiers opened volley fire.

By Thursday, July 16, the fourth day of violence, the spunk began to drain from the mob. The city had been battered, but authority, though initially ineffective, had never fully collapsed. Meanwhile, antidraft violence in other Northern cities had been swiftly crushed (one might speculate as to how today's digital communications might have incited far more widespread violence and resistance to the draft lottery). The repercussions would continue, though. The draft in New York City went largely unenforced. Efforts to arrest and indict prominent rioters were paltry to the point of irrelevance.

In the wake of Lee's defeat at Gettysburg, Southerners took heart from the Draft Riot, hoping it might portend, at last, the collapse of the Union will to continue the war, and antidraft outbursts in other areas hosting concentrations of Irish immigrants did continue to divert troops, if not on a grand scale. In this writer's home county in the Pennsylvania anthracite fields, striking mineworkers marched on the county seat (Pottsville, Schuylkill County) in the course of the "Gettysburg summer." The mob only faltered in the face of an artillery battery blocking the main road from Minersville. Ultimately, the plight of Irish mine workers (few of them better-paid skilled miners—the pits, too, had their hierarchy) would extend beyond the war years, leading to terrorism in the anthracite fields at the hands of the Molly Maguires, a secret association guilty of murder but whose purported members would hang for crimes they may not have committed, a tale still divisive today amid the now-quiet coalfields.

In the course of the Draft Riot, General Wool called for President Lincoln to declare martial law. Lincoln declined, recognizing that such a declaration would have international implications, suggesting to Southern sympathizers and fence-sitters in Europe that the Union was fragile, just as those voices hostile to the Union sought to trivialize Confederate defeats at Gettysburg and Vicksburg. In that desperate year, as the fortunes of war began to shift in the North's favor, the Union did seem politically vulnerable to many observers, foreign and domestic, but the following year, 1864, would prove the doubters wrong—amid massive bloodletting.

Nor was wartime rioting confined to the North. As early as 1862, the Richmond Bread Riot had done serious damage to the heart of the Confederate capital. On the whole, though, riots were more apt to erupt in the North because Confederate authorities, ostensibly at war to protect freedom, were far more draconian in their treatment of dissent in any form.

COPPERHEADS AND DELUSIONS

The best-known term for Northern dissenters was "Copperheads," applied to those citizens of Northern states who sympathized with the South. Most Copperheads coiled—but rarely struck—in the "West," a term then applied to border states, from Ohio through Indiana and Illinois to Missouri. Generally, the closer a community lay to the Confederacy's borders, the likelier it was to have a noisy Copperhead faction. Politically most Copperheads were "peace Democrats" in a Democratic Party split between "war Democrats," who wished to preserve the Union (without abolition), and the "peace" faction that sought peace at any price.

The true extent of the Copperhead movement remains unquantifiable, but it appears that lurid newspaper tales amplified its actual strength in the public consciousness. The Copperheads were real, but, in the course of a continent-spanning war, they provided far more sound than fury. In the border states, Republican-leaning newspapers had their offices sacked here and there, while across the Union more than three dozen military enrollment officers, tasked to compile draft-eligibility lists, were assassinated by bushwhackers or gangs. Yet, wherever local Copperheads sought to assert authority, they failed—on various occasions, veterans returning to their communities on leave banded together to beat well-known Copperheads bloody in the streets (it helped that when locally organized volunteer regiments reenlisted mid-war, the men often were granted home leaves en masse and returned eager to teach "their" Copperheads a lesson—while the Copperheads, counting on war-weariness, misjudged the mood of an increasingly committed Union military).

The Confederacy never quite knew what to make of the Copperheads. While Richmond hoped for the best from Northern dissent, there was neither a consistent policy toward nor a realistic appreciation of the Copperhead phenomenon—sometimes resulting in grim comedy. The most famous Copperhead was an Ohio politician, Clement L. Vallandigham, a rabble-rouser who had limited success in rousing the rabble. Enraged by Vallandigham's "traitorous"

speeches, Union general Ambrose Burnside ordered him arrested—
to Lincoln's embarrassment and dismay (too much has been made
of Lincoln's purported readiness to abrogate the Constitution). As
a military tribunal sentenced the Ohioan to prison for the duration
of the war, even Northern politicians who found Vallandigham odi-
ous were outraged by the army overstepping its bounds. Faced with
a media storm, local military authorities took a practical approach
to the problem and dumped Vallandigham and his suitcase at what
passed for the Confederacy's border. Expecting a hero's welcome,
Vallandigham found himself in limbo: the Confederate officers on
the scene didn't know what to do with him and, ultimately, the question passed to Richmond, where the decidedly humorless Jefferson
Davis appears to have judged Vallandigham as far too colorful and
impractical to be of use. Vallandigham continued to make mischief
where he could, but the federal military's heavy-handed treatment of
the Ohio pol proved effective, in the end, at ridding the Union of a
salient troublemaker.

At times, Copperhead plots collapsed into buffoonery. The
Confederacy certainly took an interest in fostering dissent in the
North and kept agents in Canada to spy and plot the occasional
intervention—which led to visions of burning Yankee cities that no
Copperhead had the wherewithal to burn and to ambitious invasion
plots whose results answered the 1960s question, "What if they gave
a war and nobody came?" Again and again, "parlor patriots" talked
fiercely and behaved meekly, taking Confederate funds then failing
to show up when the torches were supposed to be lit to the crackle
of firearms.

The presidential election of 1864 essentially killed the Copperhead
movement, although the corpse staggered on for a few more months.
Hoping to win the support of Union troops at the ballot box, the
Democratic Party, after a spell of bitter internal argument, nominated George McClellan, a once-popular Union general now out of
work. Then everything went wrong. McClellan stood aligned with
the war Democrats, which meant, at best, lukewarm support from
the peace Democrats. But the peace Democrats had influenced the

party platform to the extent that McClellan shied from it. Then the armies of the North began reporting a string of stunning victories: the fall of Atlanta, Cedar Creek, Mobile Bay . . . with Robert E. Lee and the South's premier army immobilized in Petersburg. The Union army's vote did not go to its old champion, McClellan, but to Lincoln: the soldiers who had endured so much could, at last, see victory ahead and did not intend to scorn it.

Yet . . . for all the ineffective, even ludicrous conspiracies concocted by the Copperheads, the war's concluding days did see the execution of the most fateful assassination plot in American history, the murder of Abraham Lincoln and the grave wounding of Secretary of State William Seward, along with botched plans to assassinate other cabinet members.

The lesson John Wilkes Booth and his coconspirators should teach us is that even madcap plots by marginal figures can change the world. After all, Gavrilo Princip was the most influential individual of the twentieth century.

RECONSTRUCTION AND REDESTRUCTION

Throughout our history, certain themes recur in different guises. One disastrous strain has been change-everything-right-now idealism. We saw it recently in well-intentioned, exuberantly naive attempts to transform deep cultures overnight in Afghanistan and Iraq, while insisting on free elections before social order had been reestablished and essential institutions emplaced. The results were corrupt, chaotic, and distinctly counterproductive as we demanded that stumbling toddlers run a marathon.

So it was with Reconstruction after the Civil War. This time, the firebrands were in the North, where vengeful legislators and an unsteady administration insisted that freed slaves be politically empowered—instantly—rather than allowing for a transition of tutelage and development. Generally, these moves were made with noble intentions that all too often veered into the gratuitously punitive where they concerned "Rebs." With the bulk of the Confederacy's national, regional, and civic leaders excluded from participation (understandably, if impractically), the door lay open for demagogical and exploitative "carpetbagger" rule as military government gave way to institutionalized Reconstruction. The federally administered Freedmen's Bureau did its best to aid the newly free, but it, too, suffered from the graft and ethical corrosion of the postwar years. For all the courage displayed by emerging Black leaders in Southern localities, they suffered ill-tutelage and exercised power only at the sufferance of self-interested or vengeful officials from the North: the selfless souls were few among the itinerant reformers. Reconstruction's downfall was only a matter of time in the humiliated, impoverished yet stubbornly proud South.

The web of local White insurrections that coalesced in the Ku Klux Klan was not inspired by outrages against White women as in *Gone with the Wind* (the most influential and most pernicious novel in American literature) but by the White experience of disenfranchisement; by the sudden overturning of social structures; and by the human tendency to cling to the sureties of tradition in times of crisis (the Taliban, al-Qaeda, ISIS, and the KKK are kin in their commitment to retrograde visions). Often led by former Confederate officers, the key operational insight of the Klansmen was that as long as they did not target the federal troops now garrisoned in the South, their intimidation of and atrocities against freed slaves often could pass with a wink or a halfhearted admonition from Union officers (this was by no means always the case, but given the political trumperies they witnessed locally, a share of Union officers felt more sympathy for their defeated fellow warriors than for the carpetbaggers and their foundering cause—nor was racial solidarity absent from the equation).

The KKK's excesses increased until, in some locales, it became the de facto arbiter of government. Klan posses were no longer scratch mobs but organized guerrilla bands—dressed not in white robes (those would come in later generations) but in outlandish spook costumes that call to mind Mardi Gras getups sewn by a disturbed seamstress. The spreading anarchy and soaring murder rate finally prompted the Grant administration to take sharp—and effective— action against the Klan. A sweeping clampdown led to thousands of arrests, although most of the accused faced only minor indispositions and even the most murderous Klan leaders never received prison sentences above five years. Still, by the mid-1870s, the remnants of the Klan were lying low.

Then a tragic miracle "saved" the South. The presidential election of 1876, fraught with extravagant corruption on all sides, resulted in a slight popular advantage for the Democratic Party but an electoral draw. Ultimately, the counting and recounting focused on Florida as shenanigans continued without resolution. Exhaustion and cynicism led, at last, to a backroom deal between the parties: Union war hero Rutherford B. Hayes would become president, but the strong-in-the-South Democratic Party got an end to Reconstruction and the removal of federal troops (other than those in regular garrisons).

Jim Crow was born.

Personally sympathetic to Blacks, "Rud" Hayes found his hands tied. A genuinely good man and popular president, he honored his campaign pledge not to seek reelection. One wonders if the dissolution of the new order for which he fought and bled on numerous battlefields influenced his decision to forgo what would have been an easy victory the second time around.

The Union had won a "great civil war," but the South won the peace to a degree that haunts us still. The Union had been preserved and slavery abolished, but justice for Black Americans would be delayed for a century and polarizing echoes of slavery linger. The North moved on to its Gilded Age, while the South retreated into bigotry, manners, and myth. Only the Spanish-American War— brilliantly managed by Hayes's wartime and political protégé, William McKinley—began to knit the not-quite-reunited United States back together, luring aged Confederate officers to don blue uniforms and serve the flag spurned in their youth. Black Americans—the Buffalo Soldiers—fought beside Theodore Roosevelt's Rough Riders at Santiago, but the glory went to the White men in campaign hats.

The KKK would reach its membership peak in the 1920s.

And yet . . . we have, after all this, endured, improved, and advanced. The lesson of this unabashedly didactic essay is that we have suffered far worse times than our moment's political shabbiness suggests. We will survive the present conceits and confusions, if not without embarrassment and scars. We are better than we have been. We are more just. The social progress in this writer's lifetime has been breathtaking and overwhelmingly positive. For all our flaws, fears, and bickering, the American dream has been opened still more widely to the many and our nightmares no longer conjure fraternal slaughter.

To study American history is to be appalled by specific events but reassured and inspired by our general progress. We, the People, are better than we know.

RECOMMENDED READING

Castel, Albert, and Thomas Goodrich. *Bloody Bill Anderson: The Short, Savage Life of a Civil War Guerrilla*. Mechanicsburg, PA: Stackpole Books, 1998.

Earle, Jonathan, and Diane Mutti Burke, eds. *Bleeding Kansas, Bleeding Missouri: The Long Civil War on the Border*. Lawrence: University Press of Kansas, 2013.

Foner, Eric. *Reconstruction: America's Unfinished Revolution, 1863–1877*. New York: Harper and Row, 1988.

Mountcastle, Clay. *Punitive War: Confederate Guerrillas and Union Reprisals*. Lawrence: University Press of Kansas, 2009.

Schecter, Barnet. *The Devil's Own Work: The Civil War Draft Riots and the Fight to Reconstruct America*. New York: Walker, 2005.

Sutherland, Daniel E., ed. *Guerrillas, Unionists, and Violence on the Confederate Home Front*. Fayetteville: University of Arkansas Press, 1999.

Weber, Jennifer L. *Copperheads: The Rise and Fall of Lincoln's Opponents in the North*. New York: Oxford University Press, 2006.

3

MILITARY DISSENT IN PEACETIME

Peter R. Mansoor

Civil–military discord is not a new phenomenon in US history; its roots go as far back as the Newburgh Conspiracy during the American Revolution, a potential coup by Continental Army officers against the Continental Congress quashed by General George Washington in an emotional meeting in March 1783. Since World War II, however, the creation of the national security state with its large standing forces has resulted in a number of clashes between military and civilian authorities, mostly regarding issues of service responsibilities such as staffing, arming, and training of the armed forces. These flare-ups have strained civil–military relations but have not ruptured them irrevocably. More recent events surrounding the 2020 presidential election, however, have proved problematic and if repeated could lead to an even more dangerous civil–military relations crisis.

THE REVOLT OF THE ADMIRALS

The end of World War II portended the traditional shrinkage of the US armed forces into small, peacetime forces with limited missions beyond homeland defense and the protection of America's trade routes and its shrinking number of overseas possessions. The emergence of the Cold War changed this dynamic in significant ways. The need to deter a strategic near-peer competitor over an extended period of time would result in more robust defense budgets and the creation of a semipermanent national security state that would significantly expand the military instrument of power.[1] Competition for defense dollars would take place under a new "national military establishment" headed by a secretary of defense who theoretically would provide oversight of the services and mitigate interservice competition for resources.[2] If that was the goal of the congressional framers of the National Security Act of 1947, the reality turned out quite differently.

One of the problems in tamping down interservice competition was the weakness of the national military establishment created by Congress. It was not a cabinet department. The secretary of defense lacked the robust staff that currently exists in the Department of Defense and "had only general, coordinating powers" over the services.[3] The service staffs of the army, navy, and newly established air force had more bureaucratic throw weight than their titular supervisor and could rely as well on congressional allies to advance their causes. The Joint Chiefs lacked both a chairman and a vice chairman. Power over roles and missions continued to reside primarily with Congress. The National Security Act of 1947 was a victory for the navy, which fought tooth and nail to prevent the unification of the services under a single uniformed chief of staff—presumably General of the Army Dwight Eisenhower.[4]

The navy had forestalled what it believed to be an army takeover of the national military establishment, but it would soon find itself engaged in what it viewed as an existential battle with the air force for the future of naval aviation—a core service function emerging from the development of fast carrier task forces that had won the Pacific War against the Imperial Japanese Navy.[5] Given their common view of the future of warfare centered on atomic weapons, both the air force and the navy desired the capability to deliver strategic nuclear weapons; the former via the development of a seventy-group program featuring the B-36 bomber, and the latter with the creation of a 65-ton supercarrier capable of launching nuclear-capable bombers. The fundamental problem was the Truman administration's insistence on restraining defense spending to balance the federal budget, while at the same time supporting a strategy of political, military, and economic competition with the Soviet Union. The defense budget, which amounted to $13.5 billion, or roughly one-third of the federal budget, was simply not large enough to accommodate all service programs. Effective lobbying by Air Force Chief of Staff General Hoyt S. Vandenberg succeeded in gaining congressional funding for the B-36 "Peacemaker" bomber, an outgrowth of a World War II proposal to create a bomber capable of reaching Germany from bases in the United States.[6] The B-36 cost six times as much as the B-29, which up to that point was the most expensive aircraft program in US history.[7]

Secretary of Defense James V. Forrestal attempted to hammer out an agreement on service roles and missions by convening a meeting of the Joint Chiefs at Key West, Florida, held March 11–14, 1948. The agreement—endorsed the next month by President Harry S. Truman and codified in a memo signed by the secretary of defense on July 1, 1948—allowed the navy an aviation arm but assigned the mission of strategic air warfare to the air force. This agreement did not solve the immediate problem, which was control of atomic weapons. The air force wanted sole control and argued against the funding of the navy's first supercarrier, the 65-ton USS *United States*. Forrestal had hoped that unification would lead to harmony, but he quickly discovered the limitations of collegiality in a budget-constrained environment.[8] A vain attempt to stop officers from criticizing other services in congressional testimony or in public came to naught.[9]

Given the limitations of his office, Forrestal lacked the power to stop the sniping among the services. The issue of interservice rivalry intensified in drafting the budget for fiscal year (FY) 1950 (which would begin on October 1, 1949). Truman wanted a defense budget no greater than $15 billion. The services drafted their separate budgets, which in July 1948 totaled a whopping $29 billion, revised downward by October to a mere $23.6 billion.[10] There simply was not enough money in Truman's defense budget to fund the military resources the services believed necessary to implement the administration's chosen strategy of deterrence and containment. Angered over Forrestal's inability to bring the Joint Chiefs to heel, concerned about his contacts with opposition candidate Thomas E. Dewey, and worried about his mental condition, Truman replaced him on March 28, 1949, with Louis Johnson, a former assistant secretary of war who came into office determined to hold the line on defense spending.[11]

Unlike the collegial Forrestal, Johnson assumed office ready to take a scalpel to the defense budget. After Truman announced a defense budget cap of $14.5 billion for FY 1951, the services once again failed to agree on a common strategy within which to frame their budget requests. As the economy went into recession, the administration, convinced that balanced budgets were the path to prosperity, cut the defense budget even further, paring $1 billion from the FY 1950 budget and reducing the FY 1951 budget to just $13 billion.[12] On April 23, Johnson canceled the construction of the USS *United States*, causing the navy secretary, John Sullivan, to resign in protest three days later.

Johnson was just getting warmed up. In July, he made further cuts to the FY 1951 budget, gutting naval aviation in the belief that carrier battle groups were of little value in wars against continental opponents and that strategic airpower provided the best deterrent against a Soviet attack. Carrier strength was halved from eight to four, and the number of carrier air groups decreased from fourteen to six. The army lost one hundred thousand soldiers, with only ten under-strength divisions on the books. Even the air force, while advantaged over the other services, was not spared. Instead of seventy air groups, the budget would allow for just forty-eight. By taking a sledgehammer to the services, Johnson had finally brought them into line with the president's budget cap.[13]

Senior naval leaders decided the time had come to go to war with the administration. Their assault featured a full-blown media blitz targeting the B-36 bomber. News stories questioned the capabilities of the massive bomber and the role of Air Force Secretary Stuart Symington in its procurement. Even before the cancellation of the USS *United States*, Cedric R. Worth, special assistant to Under Secretary of the Navy Dan A. Kimball, and Commander Thomas D. Davies, special assistant to the assistant secretary of the navy for air programs, collaborated to prepare an anonymous, nine-page paper alleging the B-36 "was a 'billion dollar blunder' whose procurement continued only because Secretary Johnson and Air Force Secretary W. Stuart Symington had personal financial stakes in its production and because they owed favors to Floyd Odlum, the head of Convair—the company manufacturing the plane."[14] The pair then leaked copies of the paper to Glenn L. Martin, chair of Convair rival Glenn L. Martin Company, and several members of Congress. Navy enthusiast Rep. James E. Van Zandt (R-PA) noisily put forward a resolution on May 25 to investigate the B-36 program. Naval supporter Rep. Carl Vinson (D-GA), alarmed at the media attention given to Van Zandt's fiery remarks, convinced the House to allow the Armed Services Committee, which he chaired, to investigate.

Hearings held in August thoroughly debunked allegations of improprieties in the procurement of the B-36. The air force also successfully defended the bomber as an important stopgap measure until the B-52 bomber was ready for production.[15] After authorship of the anonymous paper was exposed, outrage against the navy exploded. Vinson recessed the hearings on August 25 without examining the larger issues of roles and missions and the cancellation of the USS *United States*, hoping the atmosphere would cool and the issue would die.[16] It was not to be.

Two weeks later an officer on the Joint Staff, Captain John G. Crommelin, took matters into his own hands by assembling a group of reporters and lambasting the administration of the national military establishment and the ability of the army and air force to overrule navy procurement decisions. The new secretary of the navy, Francis P. Matthews, responded to the resulting publicity by issuing a classified message "directing that those who wished to express views on the matter should transmit them to him through the appropriate channels."[17] First Task Fleet commander, Vice Admiral Gerald F. Bogan, immediately did so, decrying in a memo the low morale in the navy brought on by the roles and missions controversy. Admiral Arthur W. Radford, commander in chief, Pacific Fleet, and the chief of naval operations (CNO), Admiral

Louis E. Denfeld, endorsed the memo as it made its way to the navy secretary. There matters might have stood, but on October 3, Crommelin leaked the memo and its endorsements, reigniting the media firestorm and forcing Vinson to reopen the hearings.[18]

The hearings that began on October 6 allowed the navy to present its case. Secretary Matthews rebutted allegations of low morale, attributing such comments to disgruntled naval aviators who opposed the unification of the services. Admiral Radford, speaking for the naval aviation community, "decried the morality of an atomic blitz directed against the civilian populations of major enemy cities and questioned the purported operational effectiveness of the B-36 bomber."[19] Subsequent navy witnesses claimed the B-36 was vulnerable to Soviet fighter defenses, a claim that at the time was not true.[20] The most important testimony occurred on October 13 when Admiral Denfeld broke with the administration, criticizing naval budget cuts, the cancellation of the USS *United States* in favor of the B-36, and the disregard of service views on force composition and structure. Air Force Secretary Symington and the newly installed chairman of the Joint Chiefs of Staff (CJCS), General Omar Bradley, both asserted the actions of Denfeld and other naval officers had jeopardized civilian control of the military.[21]

The "revolt of the admirals" resulted in Denfeld's immediate dismissal, but in the view of many naval officers he saved naval aviation from a descent into irrelevance. But after the revolt there was no more discussion of the navy sharing in the air force role of strategic bombing, at least not until the advent of nuclear-powered ballistic missile–carrying submarines. Johnson's budget survived the hearings, but neither it nor Johnson would survive the outbreak of the Korean War, which illustrated the weakness of the US armed services in the face of communist aggression. Massive increases in defense spending for the Korean War and the implementation of NSC-68, the blueprint for military containment of the Soviet Union, tamped down interservice rivalry after the summer of 1950.

The more important legacy of the revolt was the contemporaneous changes made to the defense establishment. Realizing the weaknesses of the loosely coordinated national military establishment, Truman had proposed a restructuring on March 5, 1949. After debate, Congress approved an amendment to the National Security Act, which Truman signed into law on August 10. The amendment consolidated the three services into a cabinet-level Department of Defense, empowered the secretary of defense with a deputy secretary and three assistant secretaries, removed the service secretaries from the National Security Council while adding the vice president, created the formal position of CJCS, and doubled the size of the Joint Staff.[22] While interservice competition for roles and missions remains a feature of the system, the days of individual services going their own way on overall defense policy were numbered.

WHO GETS TO SERVE?

Budgets have not always been the reason for military resistance to civilian authorities in peacetime. Civil rights issues have often been a source of discontent, perhaps none more so than the racial integration of the armed forces after World War II. On July 26, 1948, President Truman, concerned about America's standing in the world, supportive of the civil rights movement, and with one eye on the upcoming presidential election, issued Executive Order 9981, directing the armed services to provide equal treatment to Black service personnel. Concerned about effectiveness and reflecting the racial bias of many senior leaders, the services dragged their feet in compliance to the order. The chief of staff of the army, General Omar Bradley, believed that social evolution had made integration possible in the North, but the South "learned over the years that mixing the races was a vast problem."[23] As the president's order came out, Bradley argued against using the army as "an instrument of social change."[24]

The President's Committee on Equality of Treatment and Opportunity in the Armed Services, or the Fahy Committee, explored obstacles to integration, the most significant of which was army policy. The army had the most at stake, given that in November 1948 the percentage of Black service members amounted to 9.83 percent of the service, compared to just 6 percent for the air force, 4.3 percent for the navy, and 1.79 percent in the marine corps.[25] Army leaders pointed out that their service by law had to accept large numbers of Black draftees of lower aptitude or education than the other services. Segregation was therefore essential to maintaining the combat effectiveness of its white units, whose personnel would otherwise suffer a decline in morale and efficiency if Black soldiers were forcibly integrated among them. The problem was particularly acute among soldiers hailing from the South, who made up a high proportion of army strength.[26] Not until January 16, 1950, did the army promulgate a regulation mandating the assignment of personnel solely on the basis of skills and qualifications.[27]

The army still hedged, demanding a quota on the number of Black recruits to prevent what it considered to be the potential problem of overrepresentation of Black soldiers in the service. The Fahy Committee countered that establishing standards based on Army General Classification Test scores would be not only fair but would limit the number of Black recruits to about 10 percent of army strength, slightly below the 12 percent of Blacks in the national population.[28] On March 27, 1950, the army relented and opened recruiting without relation to race. Two months later the president disbanded the committee, considering its work done. Although the services had committed to equal treatment and opportunity, results did not match up with expectations. Army units continued to be segregated by race, resulting in a disparity of opportunities for Black soldiers. In the words of the army's official history, "much of the Army clung to old sentiments and practices and for the same old reasons."[29]

The outbreak of the Korean War and in particular the intervention of Chinese forces into the conflict in October 1950 changed the racial dynamic in the services in lasting ways. The army doubled in strength in five months, as the percentage of Black soldiers in the service rose from 10.2 percent in 1950 to 13.2 percent in December

1952. Impelled by opportunity or patriotism, Black enlistments rose during the first nine months of the war to 18 percent. These recruits poured into segregated units, causing some to be overstrength by as much as 60 percent.[30] Given this situation, commanders in Korea took matters into their own hands, assigning Black combat soldiers to fill holes in white combat units.[31] By May 14, 1951, when General Matthew B. Ridgway formally requested permission to desegregate the Eighth Army, "61 percent of Eighth Army's infantry companies were at least partially integrated."[32] When the need arose, army leaders discovered that Black soldiers could fight, sacrifice, and die as ably as white soldiers. Outside Korea the army discovered that integration did not lead to racial incidents, breakdown in discipline, lower morale, or loss of effectiveness.[33] The argument over the integration of the army, as well as the other services, had effectively ended.

The experience of the armed services with racial integration repeated itself after the end of the Cold War with the integration of gay men and women into the military, or more accurately, the open acknowledgment of their service. President Bill Clinton entered office having campaigned on a platform of allowing gays to serve in the military, but he met stiff opposition from military leaders, who advanced many of the same notions as their predecessors who opposed racial integration of the services. The Joint Chiefs of Staff and their allies in Congress, in particular the chair of the Senate Armed Services Committee, Senator Sam Nunn (D-GA), opined that allowing gays to serve openly would weaken unit cohesion and thus impair the effectiveness of the armed forces.[34] In 1993, Clinton agreed to a compromise, "Don't Ask, Don't Tell," under which gay service members would be allowed to serve provided they did not openly disclose their sexual orientation. This was little change from the previous policy, which was now enshrined in law.

Public opinion would lead to the repeal of "Don't Ask, Don't Tell" by the 111th Congress in 2010 and its replacement by legislation that allowed gay men and women to serve openly in the military. There was little pushback by military leaders, as societal attitudes toward gays had by then changed dramatically. In 1994, nearly half of Americans opposed allowing gays to serve openly in the military, a percentage that shrank to just a quarter by 2010.[35] In addition, wars in Afghanistan and Iraq increased the need for service personnel, which made discharging gay service members self-destructive. The culture wars did not end but merely shifted to other issues, such as allowing women to serve in the combat arms and allowing transgender people to serve in the military. Military leaders occasionally continue to oppose their civilian bosses on these issues, but they are not as united as they once were, reflecting the divisions in American society.

THE GOLDWATER-NICHOLS ACT

The failure of Operation Eagle Claw, the ill-fated attempt to rescue fifty-two hostages in Tehran in April 1980, as well as poor inter-service cooperation in Operation Urgent Fury, the US invasion of the island of Grenada in the Caribbean in October 1983, led to major defense reform, known as the Goldwater-Nichols Act. The postmortem on those operations showed the inability of the services to act as one when it came to procurement, training, communications, and operations. The chairman lacked real authority to override the services, which for the most part established their budgets and programs to maximize their separate capabilities without concern for interoperability with other services.[36]

Senator Nunn and Senator Barry Goldwater (R-AZ) championed reform efforts in the Senate, while Rep. William Flynt "Bill" Nichols (D-AL) led efforts in the House. The CJCS, Air Force General David Jones, as well as the army and the air force argued for reform, while Secretary of Defense Caspar Weinberger, along with the navy and the marine corps, opposed the legislation. Just as the navy had created an office to marshal arguments in opposition to the unification of the services in 1948–49 (OP-23, led by future CNO Arleigh Burke), the navy created a "War Room" to coordinate opposition to legislation mandating more "jointness" among the services. The navy's efforts failed; the Goldwater-Nichols Act passed overwhelmingly with bipartisan majorities in both chambers and was signed into law by President Ronald Reagan on October 1, 1986.[37]

The Goldwater-Nichols Act strengthened the CJCS by designating him the principal military adviser to the president, the National Security Council, and the secretary of defense, and provided him support by making the Joint Staff answerable only to the chairman. The Joint Chiefs gained a vice chairman who would oversee service procurement programs. The legislation also stripped the service chiefs of their operational responsibilities; the services would from this point forward act as force providers to combatant commanders. The chain of command would now run from the president through the secretary of defense to the combatant commanders in the field, with a coordination line through the CJCS. Officers would have to serve in a joint duty billet before being considered for promotion to flag rank. These reforms, undertaken by defense reformers in opposition to the services, strengthened the Department of Defense and the joint warfighting commands, which performed much better in the next military operations undertaken by the United States in Panama and the Gulf.[38]

A CIVIL–MILITARY RELATIONSHIP IN CRISIS

On June 1, 2020, a noisy but peaceful crowd gathered in Lafayette Square outside the White House to protest against police brutality directed at Black Americans. At around 6:30 p.m., uniformed Secret Service agents, Metropolitan Police, DC National Guard, Park Police, and personnel from other agencies used tear gas, riot shields, and batons to disperse the crowd to allow fencing to be erected around an expanded White House perimeter. Shortly after 7 p.m., President Donald Trump and a group of senior administration officials appeared and walked across the square to St. John's Episcopal

Church, where he held up a Bible in a now infamous photo op. Reporters connected the two events, but according to a subsequent Park Police investigation, they were unrelated.[39]

The appearance in the Trump delegation of a uniformed chairman of the Joint Chiefs of Staff, Army General Mark Milley, sent a problematic message that the military was supportive of Trump's "law and order" approach to the nationwide demonstrations protesting the murder of George Floyd in Minneapolis a week earlier. Furthermore, the inclusion of the chairman in what was clearly a political photo op violated a long-standing tradition of the military remaining officially apolitical. The military could not afford to get on the wrong side of this issue, as fully 40 percent of uniformed service members are people of color.[40]

The day after the Lafayette Square incident, Milley penned a message to the senior leaders of the services and the unified and specified commanders, reminding them and their subordinates of their oaths to "support and defend the Constitution and the values embedded within it" and specifically mentioning the right of free speech and assembly.[41] Ten days later in a video message to the graduating class at the National Defense University, Milley went further. "I should not have been there," Milley stated in reference to the incident. "My presence in that moment, and in that environment, created the perception of the military involved in domestic politics." He also reiterated the long-standing expectation that the military would remain aloof from politics, stating, "We must hold dear the principle of an apolitical military that is so deeply rooted in the very essence of our republic."[42]

In fact, Milley went even further in private conversations with the president. He pushed back against Trump's desire to invoke the Insurrection Act to allow federal forces to intervene in ongoing protests. One account relates that the issue led to a shouting match in the Situation Room: Trump attempted to put the chairman in charge of a military response to the protests, and Milley correctly responded that his legal responsibility was to advise, not to command. At one point Trump raised the issue of Lincoln responding with military force to rioters during the Civil War, to which Milley responded, "That guy had an insurrection. What we have, Mr. President, is a protest."[43] Five former secretaries of defense (including James Mattis, who had worked under Trump), three former chairmen of the Joint Chiefs of Staff, and a host of other voices joined in condemning the potential use of military force against protesters and riots, which had not in their view reached the level of insurrection against the federal government. Kori Schake writes, "It was a striking assertion of constitutional propriety on the military's part, and arguably the most important episode in American civil–military relations since Harry Truman fired General Douglas MacArthur for insubordination in 1951."[44]

But neither the Lafayette Square incident nor the military's reluctance to employ armed forces under the Insurrection Act to counter protests in the summer of 2020 rose to the level of insubordination to the president in the manner of MacArthur's actions in the Korean War. The next comments by General Milley might have reached that level if his words had ever been put to the test. On November 10, just four days after the election handed victory to Joe Biden, Milley received a call from an old friend who warned him about Trump acolytes and their supporters attempting to overturn the results of the election, perhaps by force. Milley was having none of it. "They may try, but they're not going to f——g succeed," Milley confided to his inner circle. "You can't do this without the military. You can't do this without the CIA and the FBI. We're the guys with the guns."[45] The Joint Chiefs also considered resigning, one after another, if Trump decided to conduct military action against their advice in the waning days of his presidency.[46] Given that Trump had fired the secretary of defense, Mark Esper, and installed a loyalist, Christopher C. Miller, in his place, the idea was not out of the question.

Milley was worried that history might be rhyming, and not in a good way. The chairman "saw parallels of Trump's rhetoric of election fraud and Adolf Hitler's insistence to his followers at the Nuremberg rallies that he was both a victim and their savior." The assault on the Capitol on January 6 could be the Trump movement's "Reichstag moment."[47] It is likely that Milley placed significant constraints on the deployment of the DC National Guard to prevent the president from invoking the Insurrection Act and using it to prevent Congress from certifying Biden's electoral victory.[48]

On January 8, Speaker of the House Nancy Pelosi called Milley to find out what he would do to prevent an unstable Trump from launching a nuclear attack or other military operations in the twelve days left in his presidency. Milley assured her that there were procedures in place to prevent an illegal, immoral, or unethical use of force. To make sure, he informed the teams in the National Military Command Center that they would inform him of any decision to use force—by the president or anyone else—before taking action. It was his "Schlesinger" moment, a reference to the actions of Secretary of Defense James Schlesinger in 1974 to prevent an imperiled (and alcoholically impaired) Richard Nixon from launching nuclear weapons as impeachment neared.[49]

Four days later, Milley gathered the Joint Chiefs together. They jointly signed a statement condemning "the assault on the U.S. Congress, the Capitol Building, and our Constitutional process."[50] The memo reaffirmed their support for the transition of government from Trump to president-elect Joe Biden on January 20. It was a reminder to the US military that their oath was to the Constitution, not to any leader, elected or otherwise. But whether the Joint Chiefs meant to or not, they had chosen sides. Ambiguities in election laws, exploited by an unscrupulous commander in chief, had resulted in the military being forced into taking a position about who had won the presidential election.[51]

On January 20, President Joe Biden assumed office in an orderly if not peaceful transition of power. Civil–military relations had been strained but remained intact. Milley had remained faithful to his oath of office, but one wonders what would have happened had the insurrection on January 6 succeeded. No doubt the resulting civil–military discord would have mirrored events much further back in time than World War II—all the way back to 1860, when the election of Republican Abraham Lincoln set in motion the succession of the South and the onset of the Civil War.

CONCLUSION

Military dissent against civilian authorities is a recurring feature of American governance. Since the creation of the national security state following the enactment of the National Security Act of 1947, military leaders have periodically publicly argued with civil authorities on issues relating to procurement, staffing, and organization—in other words, regarding elements of the armed services within the legislated purview of their uniformed leaders. Generals and admirals may have protested against the wishes of their civilian bosses, but such dissent has not seriously endangered the constitutional order of civil–military relations.

During the Trump administration, however, military dissent transcended these traditional boundaries to encompass broader questions including the nature of the relationship between the uniformed military and the president. The two most notable examples of this dynamic are the Lafayette Square incident and the transition of government after the November 2020 presidential election. As the United States enters an era in which election transitions are contested and some Americans believe that violence against the government is justified, another January 6 moment becomes likely. The armed forces will inevitably be pulled into the fray. It is incumbent upon Congress to reconsider revisions to legislation, such as the Insurrection Act and the Posse Comitatus Act, to anticipate the next civil–military crisis—for if history is any guide, there certainly will be another one.[52]

NOTES

1. M. Kent Bolton, *The Rise of the American Security State: The National Security Act of 1947 and the Militarization of U.S. Foreign Policy* (Santa Barbara, CA: Praeger, 2017).

2. Richard K. Betts, "The Durable National Security Act," *US National Security Reform: Reassessing the National Security Act of 1947*, ed. Heidi B. Demarest and Erica D. Borghard (New York: Routledge, 2019), 8–25, 12–13.

3. Allan R. Millett, Peter Maslowski, and William B. Feis, *For the Common Defense: A Military History of the United States from 1607 to 2012* (New York: Free Press, 2012), 449.

4. Millett, Maslowski, and Feis, *For the Common Defense*.

5. Clark G. Reynolds, *The Fast Carriers: The Forging of an Air Navy* (Annapolis: Naval Institute Press, 1968).

6. Daniel Ford, "B-36: Bomber at the Crossroads," *Air & Space*, April/May 1996; Michael E. Brown, *Flying Blind: The Politics of the US Strategic Bomber Program* (Ithaca, NY: Cornell University Press, 1992), 109–15.

7. Anand Toprani, "Budgets and Strategy: The Enduring Legacy of the Revolt of the Admirals," *Political Science Quarterly* 134, no. 1 (2019): 117–46, 122.

8. Toprani, "Budgets and Strategy," 126.

9. Walter Millis, ed., *The Forrestal Diaries* (New York: Viking, 1951), 516–17.

10. Toprani, "Budgets and Strategy," 128–29.

11. Less than two months later, Forrestal would commit suicide while being treated for depression. David McCullough, *Truman* (New York: Simon & Schuster, 1992), 736–40.

12. Toprani, "Budgets and Strategy," 131–32.

13. Toprani, 133–34.

14. Jeffrey G. Barlow, "Naval Aviation's Most Serious Crisis?," *Naval History Magazine* 25, no. 6 (December 2011): 38–45.

15. Jeffrey G. Barlow, *Revolt of the Admirals: The Fight for Naval Aviation, 1945–1950* (Washington, DC: Naval Historical Center, 1994), 145–57.

16. Barlow, *Revolt of the Admirals*, 226–33.

17. Barlow, "Naval Aviation's Most Serious Crisis?"

18. Barlow, "Naval Aviation's Most Serious Crisis?"

19. Barlow, "Naval Aviation's Most Serious Crisis?'

20. The B-36 flew at 40,000 feet, above the performance ceiling of existing Soviet aircraft.

21. Steven L. Rearden, *The Formative Years, 1947–1950*, vol. 1, *History of the Office of the Secretary of Defense* (Washington, DC: Historical Office, Office of the Secretary of Defense, 1984), 419.

22. Pub. L. 81-216, August 10, 1949.

23. Morris J. MacGregor, Jr., *Integration of the Armed Forces, 1940–1965* (Washington, DC: Center of Military History, 2001), 229.

24. MacGregor, *Integration of the Armed Forces*, 317.

25. MacGregor, 326.

26. MacGregor, 350–51.

27. US Army Special Regulation 600-629-1, *Utilization of Negro Manpower in the Army* (Washington, DC: Department of the Army, 16 January 1950).

28. MacGregor, *Integration of the Armed Forces*, 372.

29. MacGregor, 430.

30. MacGregor, 430.

31. MacGregor, 433.

32. MacGregor, 434.

33. MacGregor, 456.

34. Alejandro de la Garza, "'Don't Ask, Don't Tell' Was a Complicated Turning Point for Gay Rights: 25 Years Later, Many of the Same Issues Remain," *Time*, July 19, 2018.

35. Garza, "'Don't Ask, Don't Tell.'"

36. James R. Locher III, *Victory on the Potomac: The Goldwater-Nichols Act Unifies the Pentagon* (College Station: Texas A&M University Press, 2002), chap. 1.

37. John J. Hamre, "Reflections: Looking Back at the Need for Goldwater-Nichols," Center for Strategic and International Studies, January 27, 2016, https://www.csis.org/analysis/reflections-looking-back-need-goldwater-nichols.

38. Locher, epilogue to *Victory on the Potomac.*

39. Tom Jackman and Carol D. Leonnig, "Report: Park Police Didn't Clear Lafayette Square Protesters for Trump Visit," *Washington Post*, June 9, 2021.

40. Kim Parker, Anthony Cilluffo, and Renee Stepler, "6 Facts about the US Military and Its Changing Demographics," Pew Research Center, April 13, 2017, https://www.pewresearch.org/fact-tank/2017/04/13/6-facts-about-the-u-s-military-and-its-changing-demographics.

41. Memorandum, CJCS to the Joint Force, June 2, 2020, https://www.jcs.mil/Portals/36/Documents/CJCS%20Memo%20to%20the%20Joint%20Force%20(02JUN2020).pdf.

42. General Mark Milley's Keynote Address to National Defense University Class of 2020 Graduates, June 11, 2020, YouTube video, 13:13, https://www.youtube.com/watch?v=7AKmmApwioM.

43. Matthew Brown, "Gen. Mark Milley, Donald Trump at Odds over Crackdown on 2020 Racial Justice Protests, Book Reveals," *USA Today*, June 28, 2021. The cited account is Matthew Bender, *Frankly, We Did Win This Election: The Inside Story of How Trump Lost* (New York: Twelve, 2021).

44. Kori Schake, "The Military and the Constitution Under Trump," *Survival* 62, no. 4 (July 22, 2020): 31–38.

45. Carol Leonnig and Philip Rucker, *I Alone Can Fix It: Donald J. Trump's Catastrophic Final Year* (New York: Penguin, 2021), chap. 17.

46. Leonnig and Rucker, *I Alone Can Fix It.*

47. Leonnig and Rucker, chap. 20.

48. Ryan Goodman and Justin Hendrix, "Crisis of Command: The Pentagon, the President, and January 6," *Just Security*, December 21, 2021.

49. Bob Woodward and Robert Costa, *Peril* (New York: Simon & Schuster, 2021), xix–xxvii; Dakota S. Rudesill, "Nuclear Command and Statutory Control," *Journal of National Security Law & Policy* 11, no. 2 (March 12, 2021): 365–434, 379.

50. Joint Chiefs of Staff, Message to the Joint Force, January 12, 2020, https://www.jcs.mil/Portals/36/Documents/JCS%20Message%20to%20the%20Joint%20Force%20JAN%2012%2021.pdf.

51. I am grateful to Dakota S. Rudesill for this insight. For more on the ambiguity of election laws and what can be done to fix them, see Dakota S. Rudesill, "Preventing a Military Decision About Who Won a Disputed Election," *Just Security*, October 29, 2020.

52. For a discussion of how these statutes can be amended to anticipate future civil crises, see Mark Nevitt, "2022 Update: Good Governance Paper No. 6: Domestic Military Operations," *Just Security*, January 25, 2022.

RECOMMENDED READING

Barlow, Jeffrey G. *Revolt of the Admirals: The Fight for Naval Aviation, 1945–1950.* Washington, D.C.: Naval Historical Center, 1994.

Leonnig, Carol, and Philip Rucker, *I Alone Can Fix It: Donald J. Trump's Catastrophic Final Year.* New York: Penguin, 2021.

Locher, James R. III, *Victory on the Potomac: The Goldwater-Nichols Act Unifies the Pentagon.* College Station: Texas A&M University Press, 2002.

MacGregor, Morris J., Jr., *Integration of the Armed Forces, 1940–1965.* Washington: Center of Military History, 2001.

Millett, Allan R., Peter Maslowski, and William B. Feis, *For the Common Defense: A Military History of the United States from 1607 to 2012.* New York: Free Press, 2012.

Woodward, Bob, and Robert Costa, *Peril.* New York: Simon & Schuster, 2021.

4

THE COLD WAR, AMERICAN ISOLATIONISM, AND THE KOREAN WAR

Williamson Murray

There are events in history where decisions take the future and twist it in substantially different directions or provide certain trends with an entirely new emphasis. The outbreak of the Korean War, which would impact the course that the United States would pursue over the next four decades until the collapse of the Soviet Union, represents an example of such an event. To understand the importance of the war, this paper aims to lay out the period leading up to June 1950 and where the Americans and their Communist opponents seem to have been heading. It will then turn to how the North Korean invasion of the south profoundly altered the course the United States would pursue as well as its approach to equipping its military and preparing for war. We will also examine the unintended effects that act of aggression would have on the future history of the balance of power in Asia.

THE BACKGROUND

The ending of World War II left the United States and the Soviet Union as the two great powers in the world. They stood at opposite ends of the ideological spectrum, and in retrospect there was every prospect of a great war between the two powers, especially considering their ideological orientations. But two crucial factors mitigated against that possibility and prevented the outbreak of World War III, a war that would have been even more destructive than World War II. With the use of nuclear weapons such a conflict might well have destroyed civilization. But at least in terms of his willingness to take risks, Stalin was not Adolf Hitler. Unlike the German dictator, who believed only he could prevent the victory of international Jewry, Stalin, as a convinced Communist, believed he had history on his side and that the capitalist world would inevitably collapse.

Moreover, unlike most in the West and certainly those in charge of Nazi Germany in 1941, Stalin understood the disparity between the economic strengths of his nation and those of the United States, especially considering the extraordinary damage the *Wehrmacht* had inflicted on the western portions of the Soviet Union. World War II had underlined for Stalin the economic strength of the United States. Lend-Lease had proved crucial not only in preventing mass starvation but in providing support to Soviet industry and military forces. Khrushchev in his memoirs quotes the dictator as having commented to his colleagues shortly after the war that the Soviet Union would not have defeated Nazi Germany without the economic and military aid that the United States had provided his regime: "If we had had to fight Nazi Germany one on one, we could not have stood up against Germany's pressure and we would have lost the war."[1]

The second factor influencing Stalin was the dropping of the atomic bomb on the Japanese by the Americans over Hiroshima and Nagasaki in August 1945 and the almost immediate surrender of the Japanese. As he bemoaned to his entourage: "Brains—and the military technology they could now produce—now counted for just as much as the divisions with which the Red Army had occupied Eastern Europe."[2] Even with the explosion of the first Soviet nuclear device in 1949, that basic reality was not to change over the course of the Cold War. Behind the threat of the use of conventional military force would stand the dark visage of nuclear war. Moreover, Stalin's visit to Germany to attend the Potsdam Conference had provided the dictator with an indication of the terrible damage Anglo-American conventional air power had inflicted on Germany's industry and infrastructure, even without the use of nuclear weapons.

If the fear of American nuclear weapons deterred Stalin from undertaking too aggressive a military policy, it certainly did not deter the dictator from strategic and diplomatic policies, supported at times by his puppets, that threatened Iran, Turkey, and Greece and attempted to sabotage Western policies politically and economically toward the conquered Germans. The result was a steady deterioration of relations between the Soviet Union on one side and the Americans on the other. There were significant warnings from those intelligent enough to see the danger signs in terms of Soviet behavior.

Yet we should not underestimate the immense goodwill that the terrible struggle the Soviets and the Red Army had waged against the Nazi invaders had built up among the American people—a reservoir of favorable attitudes that the American government had encouraged throughout the conflict.[3] Moreover, the American people had just come through the exhausting and costly experience of World War II, and there was little enthusiasm for an active foreign policy, especially considering the deep thread of isolationism that had run through the American public since its founding. Even Roosevelt, with his idealistic hopes for cooperation among nations and America's participation in that effort, had commented to Stalin that he did not believe American troops would remain in Europe for more than a couple of years.

Indeed, there were strong tendencies in America that were pushing against any policy of containment of the Soviet Union. On the left stood the likes of Henry Wallace and other fellow travelers. The ideological struggle against fascism that had marked much of the Left's *Weltanschauung* in the 1930s still remained, even if considerably damaged by the Nazi-Soviet Non-Aggression Pact of August 1939. On the right stood steadfast isolationists, particularly in the Midwest, who believed the United States had no business in participating in the messy politics of Europe. They, of course, had remained steadfast opponents of America's participation in the European war until the shattering impact of Pearl Harbor, followed shortly thereafter by a German declaration of war.

Churchill's speech at Westminster College in Missouri in March 1946 was a clear depiction of the reality that the West confronted, but it did not receive enthusiastic support in either the United States or the United Kingdom. His wonderful depiction that "from Stettin on the Baltic to Trieste on the Adriatic, an iron curtain has descended across the continent" finds more of an echo today than it did at the time. Along the same lines, thirteen days before Churchill's speech, George Kennan, then deputy chief of mission in the American embassy in Moscow, had dispatched his famous long cable to the State Department from Moscow. In it he argued that the United States needed to follow "a long-term, patient, but firm and vigilant *containment* of Russian expansive tendencies." That cable would appear the next year in July 1948 in the famous "Mr. X" article. Yet if Kennan found support among a number of senior policy makers like the secretary of defense, James Forrestal, it would take a considerable period of time to work its way through the rabbit warrens of the American government.

Stalin would help enormously in disabusing many of those who held isolationist views by the actions that he would take. But it would take a number of Soviet moves to persuade the Americans to start on their journey to contain the Soviets. Given the desperate economic and political situation that World War II had inflicted on Western Europe, George Marshall suggested to President Harry Truman in June 1947 that the Americans should announce what he termed as the European Recovery Act, later known as the Marshall Plan. But it almost immediately ran into substantial opposition from isolationists in Congress, and there were indications that it might not pass.

But in February 1948, the Czech Communists, supported by the Soviets, overthrew the remains of the democratic Beneš government of Czechoslovakia. The motivation for the Soviet action appears to have been more a desire to solidify Stalin's control over Eastern Europe rather than an overt move against the West. Nevertheless, the coup, which overthrew the democratically elected Czech government, was perceived by many in Washington as the first step toward Soviet efforts to overthrow governments in the West. Thus, the coup played a considerable role in persuading Congress to pass the European Recovery Act, which underlined that American isolationism was beginning to collapse in the face of the reality of the international scene.

Tensions remained high in Europe. Four months after the Czech coup, the Soviets imposed a blockade of the Western sectors of Berlin. Here again, Stalin's action was driven largely by concerns internal to the control of his empire. East Germany, which the Soviet dictator was hoping to create as a counterweight to the emerging unification of the occupation zones controlled by the Western powers, was hemorrhaging population that threatened its political stability. Thus, the move seemingly provided two advantages: strengthening East Germany and providing an easy political victory over the Western Powers.

However, Stalin had miscalculated. The Anglo-American response was the great airlift that supplied the city's population with the coal and sustenance sufficient to survive. Eleven months later Stalin called the blockade off in one of the more humiliating political defeats of his career. The Berlin blockade also strengthened the perception among many in the United States that the Soviet Union represented an existential threat as had Germany and Japan a decade earlier.

By this point it was clear that the Western-occupied zones in Germany were not only drawing more closely together politically but were also making a substantial economic recovery. Perhaps even more alarming to the Soviets was the fact that the Western European states were forming a series of political and economic alliances, the most important of which in April 1949 led to the creation of the North Atlantic Treaty Organization (NATO), which included the United States, Canada, and Iceland as well as the European states.

From a Western perspective, the problem was that there were few teeth behind the alliance. The Europeans possessed neither the economic strength nor the willingness to embark on major programs of rearmament unless they received substantial amounts of military aid from the United States. And that was certainly not to be forthcoming as long as the American military remained in the demobilized status that had ensued at the end of World War II. And despite its increasingly hostile foreign policy toward the Soviets, the Truman administration displayed little interest in increasing defense spending. If anything, the response among the president and policy makers in Washington was to make further cuts in the defense budget.

And the rebuilding of the massive American military establishment in 1945 that it had so ruthlessly disarmed in the aftermath of World War II was going to require a major effort. From a level of 11,365,000 men and women serving in the services in August 1945, the American military had declined to 2,874,000 by 1947.[4] Gone were the fleets of aircraft carriers, the wings of bombers, the eighty-nine army and six marine divisions that had contributed to the destruction of Nazi Germany and Imperial Japan. What was left was indeed a hollow military force, the heart of which lay entirely in American possession of the atomic bomb.[5] Moreover, the Soviets, helped enormously by spies within the American and British scientific establishments, had exploded their own bomb in 1949, although they possessed as of then no capability to deliver nuclear weapons beyond the immediate spaces surrounding their empire.

Thus, virtually all of America's strategic eggs were in the basket filled with nuclear weapons. The initial Strategic Air Command (SAC) Emergency War Plan I-49 posited using all 133 atomic weapons in American possession to attack seventy Soviet cities—if they could be found.[6] Those nuclear weapons were not in the hands of the United States Air Force but rather in the hands of the Atomic Energy Commission. Moreover, the B-29s and crews that were supposed to execute the plan were not prepared for their purported mission. It was doubtful whether they would have been able to find their targets in anything other than perfect weather conditions. Nevertheless, the code name for the initial American plan for nuclear war was titled "To Destroy a Nation." The planners characterized their effort as representing "an opportunity to put warfare on an economic, sensible, reasonable basis."[7] The problem was that "To Destroy a Nation" hardly represented a reasonable strategic approach to those who thought seriously about deterring the Soviets.

In March 1950, Paul Nitze led a study group combined of senior officials from the Defense and State Departments to produce NSC (National Security Council) 68. Nitze's focus was on preparing the United States and its military to meet what he characterized as aiming at the overthrow of America's allies. Soviet military power, now augmented with the possession of the atomic bomb, represented an existential threat not only to its European allies but also to the United States itself.[8] In political terms, Nitze noted that the Soviets were aiming at establishing "domination of the European land mass."[9]

Not surprisingly, in direct contravention of the Truman defense budgets over the past several years, Nitze's report underlined that the administration was simply not providing the military forces necessary to back up its foreign policy. Thus, NSC 68 recommended a tripling of the defense budget with all three services receiving major new allocations to build up US conventional as well as nuclear capabilities. Nitze's program also urged significant military aid to America's allies, particularly in Europe, which were directly threatened by Soviet military forces.

In fact, there was little chance of Congress passing NSC 68 due to liberal opposition to defense outlays and solid isolationism among many Midwestern members of Congress who opposed moves that suggested an American commitment to Europe. Moreover, Truman himself was not about to support any such program of massive rearmament, given his emphasis on balancing the budget. Thus, the defense budget for the coming fiscal year of 1951 confronted substantial cuts in the entire force structure. Despite the threatening international situation, the United States was not going to begin a serious program of rearmament. Again, as with Pearl Harbor, America's opponents came to its rescue.

THE KOREAN WAR

At the end of June 1950, the North Koreans invaded South Korea. Admittedly, the American secretary of state, Dean Acheson, had indicated in a speech in January of that year that both South Korea and Taiwan lay beyond America's defense perimeter. One suspects, however, that Acheson's speech only peripherally influenced Kim Il-sung to launch the invasion. Kim had been pestering the Soviet dictator since early 1949 for permission to launch his well-prepared army against the South Koreans. What strengthened his desire to mount a conventional invasion was the fact that the South Koreans with American support had largely crushed North Korean efforts to wage a guerrilla war in the south.[10]

Stalin, however, feared that an invasion of South Korea by Kim's forces could lead to war between the Soviet Union and the United States. In discussion with the North Koreans, he demanded that they consult with the Chinese Communists. They in turn suggested that Kim wait until they had completed the conquest in Taiwan.[11] In April 1950, when Kim met with the Soviet dictator, he indicated that he did not expect the Americans to intervene and that Mao had promised military aid if needed.

Moreover, Kim assured Stalin that the invasion would take no longer than a week, aided by the support of two hundred thousand guerrillas in the south. Still, not entirely convinced, Stalin asked the Koreans to get firm assurances from Mao that the Chinese would support the invasion. At a further meeting with their Chinese counterparts in Beijing, the Koreans received the assurance that the Chinese Communists would stand by their North Korean comrades, although Mao expressed considerable doubt about Kim's optimistic assurances.[12]

In the end it was Joseph Stalin who supplied not only the military wherewithal for the invasion but the green light that allowed the North Koreans to move against the South. From what we know about Stalin, it is likely that he viewed the North Korean invasion of the South as an opportunity to test American resolve. Had there been no American response, he would undoubtedly have undertaken further moves in Europe, the most obvious an invasion of Yugoslavia, which had broken away from the Soviet bloc. In retrospect, the North Korean invasion of South Korea would prove to be one of the most serious mistakes of Stalin's career.

Even before the invasion, Mao Zedong and his army were preparing to intervene in Korea, should it prove necessary. The expectation among the North Koreans was that the invasion would prove a cakewalk, particularly since the Americans had prepared the South Korean army almost exclusively to fight against the indigenous guerrillas that the North had been arming and sending south. Two surprises awaited the Communists: the South Koreans put up far greater resistance than expected, while the popular uprising that the invaders expected simply failed to occur. The Republic of Korea put up considerable resistance, especially considering how lightly its troops were armed. In fact, the number of atrocities the North Koreans perpetrated undoubtedly solidified the South's support behind the Syngman Rhee regime. Moreover, while the Soviets had prepared the North Koreans in arms and training for combat, they had not prepared them logistically for the problem of driving down the hill-strewn Korean Peninsula. Moreover, American air power was soon ravaging the supply lines of the North Koreans as they drove ever farther into South Korea.

The second great surprise was undoubtedly the American response, which almost immediately committed the United States to the fight on the Korean Peninsula. From an initial set of air strikes to the commitment of occupation troops from Japan to the movement of troops and military equipment from the United States, the American reaction was fierce and effective.[13] Despite having disarmed to a considerable extent, the military was able to draw on the vast expertise of those veterans who had been demobilized in 1945. Nor was there any shortage of military equipment. Yet in the larger framework of American strategy in response to the North Korean invasion, the

war in Asia remained of lesser importance than meeting the immediate military threat of a Soviet invasion of Western Europe, which
American leaders believed was in the offing.

The North Korean invasion was to see Douglas MacArthur at his
best and worst. His contribution to the rebuilding of Japan represents
one of the great strategic and political moves in American history.
Almost singlehandedly he prevented a mass starvation from occurring on the Japanese Home Islands at the end of 1945 by forcing
Washington to undertake major shipments of food.[14] His response
to the invasion of South Korea was measured and intelligent. The
amphibious landing at Inchon with the 1st Marine Division against
the advice of virtually everyone in the military and in Washington
represents one of the great strokes of operational art. It completely
undermined Chairman of the JCS Omar Bradley's comment that
amphibious landings were a thing of the past.

Thereafter, MacArthur's performance was dreadful. His underestimate of China's willingness to intervene in the Korean War as
well as the potential military strength of the People's Liberation
Army (PLA), followed by a desperate overestimation of Chinese
military strength, represented serious mistakes at the political and
strategic levels. The result was the catastrophic retreat from the Yalu
that destroyed two South Korean divisions and wrecked an American
division. Moreover, the general now overestimated Chinese capabilities as the Communists approached the 38th Parallel despite the
extraordinary logistic difficulties they had in keeping their troops
supplied under the massive pounding they were receiving from
American air attacks.

MacArthur then caused the greatest civil–military confrontation
in the US government since the McClellan-Lincoln controversy. In
March, relations between the general and the president reached the
breaking point. Challenging the administration's policy that empha-
sized concerns for European security over those of the Pacific, on
March 24, 1951, MacArthur issued a communique that "widely
exceeded his part record of direct challenges to his superiors."[15]
Twelve days later a Republican congressman read a letter from the

general into the Congressional Record that severely criticized the president for his emphasis on a European-first strategy and refusing to recognize that it was Asia where the United States should place its emphasis. That was more than enough of MacArthur's insolence for Truman. The next day Truman fired the general, thus ending a military career that had spanned five decades.

What MacArthur failed to see was the larger strategic framework. In 1950, Western Europe represented a greater American strategic interest than what was happening in Asia. As Omar Bradley correctly pointed out, an extension of the Korean War to China would be the "wrong war, in the wrong place, at the wrong time." Truman's relief of MacArthur represented the right strategic and political decision, although it caused the unpopular president a great deal of unjustified, bad publicity. To all intents and purposes, it ended the general's career as he "faded away into obscurity."

THE FALLOUT FROM THE WAR

The most important impact of the Korean War was that it fundamentally changed America's defense policies and priorities. Above all, it made the recommendations of NSC 68 a reality. In September 1950, the defense budget would posit an increase in force structure from four aircraft carriers to twelve; the ten understrength and underequipped army divisions were to increase to seventeen combat ready divisions and seventeen regimental combat teams; and an air force would see its force structure increase to seventy wings. The army's personnel strength would rise from 630,000 before the war to 1,263,000; naval personnel from 461,000 to 717,818; and air force personnel from 416,000 to 688,186.[16]

The Korean War led almost immediately to a major commitment of US troops to the defense of Western Europe. The flow of those reinforcements across the Atlantic began as soon as the first trained draftees had formed into military units. Altogether the Korean War led Truman to call 806,000 reservists and national guardsmen to active duty, while issuing draft calls for 585,000 draftees. Ironically, the draftees filled out the new army divisions and for the most part were sent to Europe. The reservists, mostly combat veterans of World War II, were sent to Korea. Altogether defense spending increased to $56.2 billion for fiscal year 1951 and to $70 billion for the following two years.

All in all, the Korean War involved a greater expenditure of funds in its first year than the total prewar defense budget had cost. In effect Korea created an armed nation that would remain so, with some ups and downs, to the end of the Cold War. Among other items that now helped to explode the defense budget was the allocation of $1,400,000,000 to increase by an order of magnitude America's nuclear capabilities.[17]

The Korean War would also have a major impact on the political framework of the United States. Among other effects, given that the war on the peninsula settled down to a murderous stalemate, it would make Truman one of the most unpopular presidents in American history. One of the effects of the Korean War was to exacerbate the already anticommunist rhetoric that was marking American politics. It created an intense anticommunist hostility in the body politic, the most obvious of which was Senator Joseph McCarthy, who would carry out what many have regarded as a witch hunt for Communists and fellow travelers in the federal government.

In fact, a number of Republicans had seized on the fall of Chiang Kai-shek's Nationalist regime to lambast the Democrats as being responsible for the takeover of the Chinese mainland. Along with the slogan of "who lost China" went arguments that President Roosevelt had surrendered Eastern Europe to the none-too-tender mercies of Stalin.[18] But the anticommunist crusade really got going when Senator McCarthy attacked Secretary of State Dean Acheson for shielding no fewer than 205 Communists in the State Department. The senator's numbers were fictitious, but they soon gained traction throughout Congress and American society.

The outbreak of the Korean War only served to exacerbate what eventually became a witch hunt. In fact, those few individuals who were identified in the early 1950s were either small fish who had little opportunity to damage national security or nonexistent spies hiding in the bowels of the State Department and Pentagon. In retrospect, most of those among the intellectuals and in the arts identified by the various efforts of House Un-American Activities Committee (HUAC) and McCarthy deserved punishment not so much for the damage they did to national security but for their obdurate stupidity as fellow travelers in supporting Joseph Stalin's murderous tyranny throughout the 1930s and World War II.

There is a tendency to believe that the Soviet agents who burrowed into the American government did substantial damage to American national security by the information they passed along to the Soviets. And in fact they did cause serious damage, but by 1950 they had been identified. Certainly, the Soviet agents who passed along critical information on what was occurring in the Manhattan Project did extraordinary harm to the nation for whom they were supposedly working. In the end, though, those individuals had either turned state's evidence or were on the way to the electric chair or had fled to the embrace of Soviet-held territory.

Unfortunately, the really serious damage to American foreign policy and interests had occurred during World War II. Two figures stand out for their mendacious betrayal of their country. Both held positions of trust at the highest level: Alger Hiss and Harry Dexter White, the guilt of both of whom has been largely established by the Venona tapes. That Hiss was a Soviet agent, there is no doubt. Yet, in retrospect, Hiss's position was largely advisory, and it is unclear how much damage he was able to cause in the advice he tendered to his superiors about how they might best deal with the Soviets. The reality for the most part lies buried in unrecorded words. Nevertheless, Hiss was in a position to offer the worst sort of advice to the senior people he served, including the secretary of state and the president.

The case with White is clearer. In 1944, as Secretary of the Treasury Henry Morgenthau Jr.'s chief aide, White blocked a major financial grant to the Chinese Nationalists, which might have stabilized that government's financial difficulties; the resulting financial collapse played a major role in the Communist success in overthrowing Chiang's regime. But perhaps even more important was that during the war, White was able to ensure that the British would have to pay the highest possible interest on the loans that their straightened financial circumstances forced them to ask for from the United States and would force them to sell off substantial portions of their financial capital. At the same time, he was ensuring that the Soviets would have to pay minimal interest on the loans they were receiving.

Finally, we might note that White was a major author of the Morgenthau Plan for postwar Germany. Admittedly the plan was sabotaged by leaks, but had it been executed, it would have ruined any chance of including the Germans in the Western alliance. As it was, the Morgenthau Plan provided Goebbels with a wonderful tool to persuade the German people to see the war through to the bitter end. It did not, however, actually extend the war, because the German people were already confirmed in their desire to continue the hopeless struggle. The war would have continued until May 1945, even had the Morgenthau Plan not existed.

THE UNINTENDED EFFECTS

The eventual armistice that ended the Korean War created a standoff in which South Korea managed to maintain a small piece of North Korea, but the two Koreas would remain separated. In the long term, a vibrant, democratic economic powerhouse would emerge in the south, while North Korea would become a pariah state that has not been able to feed its own people for substantial periods of time. Certainly, the former was a surprise, given the massive damage the war had inflicted on the South Korean people and the nation's infrastructure.

One of the most important unintended effects of the Korean War was the impact it had on China's geographic and strategic position. Mao and his murderous followers had solidified their hold on

Mainland China in 1949. In March 1950, they launched an amphibious assault to drive the Kuomintang off Hainan Island. Major fighting lasted until May, when the island finally was fully under the control of the PLA. Next on Mao's list was clearly Taiwan, but that represented a considerably harder nut to crack; not only was it farther from the mainland, but Chiang had managed to concentrate the remains of his military forces on the island.

The invasion of South Korea changed entirely the political, strategic, and military framework of Asia. Four days after the invasion of South Korea, Truman ordered that the Seventh Fleet now guard the straits between Taiwan and the mainland. That decision put paid to any ideas the PLA had of making a successful amphibious assault on the Nationalist stronghold—a situation that has continued into the twenty-first century. In terms of the PLA military and strategic problems, the existence of Taiwan as an independent entity, now a democratic one, has solidified the great island chain running from Japan through Taiwan to the Philippines and on into Malaysia and Indonesia that represents a significant hindrance to Chinese control of the Eastern Pacific. The extraordinary lengths that the current regime in Beijing has taken to force the Taiwanese government to roll over politically underlines just how valuable the island nation is to the strategic interests of the United States and its allies in East Asia.

Equally important was the fact that the Korean War would create the framework of research and development that would lead Dwight Eisenhower to create DARPA (Defense Advanced Research Projects Agency). In the long run that increased funding for defense projects would lead to the enormous advantage the United States would enjoy over the Soviet Union by the end of the Cold War. We should also note that the Korean War created a vibrant American military commitment to the defense of Western Europe. In other words, it put real military teeth into the NATO alliance and the policy of containment of the Soviet Union. Politically the presence of substantial numbers of American troops in Germany made the rearmament of West Germany palatable to its neighbors, particularly the French.

One of the few negative aspects of the American response to the invasion of South Korea was the decision to provide the French with substantial military aid for the colonial war they were waging against the ruthless Communist Viet Minh in South Vietnam. At the time the Viet Minh were close to driving the French out. American aid would continue the French effort for another four years. Tragically, the increasing US support for the French would step by step lead to the disastrous American intervention in the civil war in South Vietnam in the early 1960s. In the larger sense, the American decision to help the French reflected the mistaken belief that the emerging Communist nations represented a unified threat. That belief would significantly impact America's strategic approach in the 1950s and 1960s.

NOTES

1. Nikita Khrushchev, *Memoirs of Nikita Khrushchev*, vol. 1, *Commissar, 1918–1945* (College Park: Penn State University Press, 2005), 675–76.

2. Joseph Stalin quoted in Adam B. Ulam, *Expansion and Coexistence: The History of Soviet Foreign Policy, 1917–67* (New York: Frederick A. Praeger, 1968), 403–4.

3. Ironically, we now know that the Germans devoted a greater percentage of their resources to the defense of the Reich against the Combined Bomber Offensive that Bomber Command of the Royal Air Force and Eighth and Fifteenth Air Forces of the US Army Air Forces waged against Germany. Phillips Payson O'Brien argues that from 1943 on over 60 percent of German resources went to the production of aircraft and antiaircraft weapons and ammunition. Phillips Payson O'Brien, *How the War Was Won: Air-Sea Power and Allied Victory in World War II* (Cambridge: Cambridge University Press, 2015), 484.

4. Ulam, *Expansion and Coexistence*, 403–4.

5. For the state of the US Air Force in the late 1940s, see Williamson Murray, "The United States Air Force: The Past as Prologue," in *America's Defense*, ed. Michael Mandelbaum (New York: Holmes & Meier, 1989).

6. And given the navigational capabilities of the time, that was a doubtful proposition.

7. Stephen Budiansky, *Code Warriors: NSA's Codebreakers and the Secret Intelligence War against the Soviet Union* (New York: Knopf, 2016), 123.

8. Melvyn P. Leffler, *A Preponderance of Power: National Security, the Truman Administration, and the Cold War* (Stanford, CA: Stanford University Press, 1992), chap. 8.

9. Leffler, *Preponderance of Power*, 355.

10. For the guerrilla war before June 1950, see particularly Allan R. Millett, *The War for Korea, 1945–1950: A House Burning* (Lawrence: University Press of Kansas, 2005).

11. Chen Jian, *Mao's China & the Cold War* (Chapel Hill: University of North Carolina Press, 2001), 54.

12. Millett, *War for Korea, 1945–1950*, 244.

13. For the most thorough examination of the Korean War that examines the conflict from the Korean, American, and Chinese perspectives, see Allan R. Millett, *The War for Korea, 1950–1951: They Came from the North* (Lawrence: University Press of Kansas, 2010). See also T. R. Fehrenbach's history of the war: *This Kind of War: The Classic Korean War History* (Washington, DC: Brassey's, 2001).

14. Richard Frank, "Truman and MacArthur: Their Rendezvous with History," in *High Commands and Grand Strategy in War*, eds. Williamson Murray and James Lacey (forthcoming, 2023).

15. Richard B. Frank, *MacArthur: A Biography* (New York: St. Martin's Press Griffin, 2007), 161.

16. Leffler, *Preponderance of Power*, 373.

17. Leffler, *Preponderance of Power*, 373.

18. In fact, at the time the Yalta agreement was negotiated, Soviet troops were almost to Berlin, while American and British troops had yet to cross the Rhine.

5

AMERICAN OBJECTIVES IN WAR AND DISSENT WITHIN THE MILITARY

Bing West

America is the most powerful country in the history of the world, yet it has not won even one of the three major wars it has fought over the past half century. This has not been due to a lack of effort and persistence. Our troops fought in Vietnam for nine years, in Iraq for a dozen, and for twenty years in Afghanistan. But no sensible person would claim that the results in those three countries were worth the costs in American casualties, money, and global influence. In Vietnam, Iraq, and Afghanistan, America failed in its objective to develop and sustain democracies.

Why did this happen, and why was there not effective dissent from within the senior military ranks that would force change, when the military strategies were failing, year after year? And what are the implications going forward, given that Russia's invasion of Ukraine threatens the international order that has so well served the interests of America and the West since the fall of the Soviet Union?

HISTORICAL CONTEXT

Before Vietnam, no clear precedent concerning military dissent had emerged from the two world wars and the Korean "police action." During World War I, President Wilson was not involved in military strategy, to the delight of General Pershing, the commander of US forces in France. Wilson, remaining distant from strategic decision making, encountered no instance of disagreement with the military. Conversely, during World War II President Roosevelt was so inextricably involved with the military high command that all critical decisions reflected common agreement. Disputes about strategy, especially the allocation of forces to the European versus Pacific theater, were frequent. But the strategic goal—unconditional surrender—and the operations did not evoke any serious dissent.

In contrast, both before and during the Korean War (1950–53), President Truman encountered instances of grave military dissent. In the first case, in 1949 the secretary of defense canceled construction of the navy's "supercarrier" because the mission of the strategic nuclear bomber fleet had been assigned to the fledgling US Air Force, created by legislation only two years earlier. The navy rebelled, resulting in twelve days of congressional hearings. Army General Omar Bradley, chairman of the Joint Chiefs of Staff, accused the navy of being in "open rebellion against the civilian control." Naval officials, he said, were "'fancy dans' who won't hit the line with all they have on every play unless they can call the signals." Congress did not fund the carrier and President Truman forced the resignation of the chief of naval operations (CNO).

Truman won that battle, only to lose the next. In addition to the navy, the president disliked the US Marine Corps, and he supported eliminating it as a separate service. In 1950, he wrote, "the Marine Corps is the Navy's police force and as long as I am President that is what it will remain. . . . They have a propaganda machine almost the equal of Stalin's. . . . The Chief of Naval Operations is the Chief of Staff of the Navy of which the Marines are a part." The phrase "Navy's police force" ignited a public furor, given the marines' epic battles like Iwo Jima during World War II. Worse still for Truman, his disparaging view of the marine corps was issued just two weeks before the marine amphibious landing at Inchon, which turned the tide in the Korean War. Like the navy, the marines appealed to Congress to write into law their existence as a separate armed service, with specific roles and missions. Unlike the navy, the marines conducted their lobbying quietly. Truman could not accuse them of open insubordination, let alone fire the commandant of the marine corps, as he had the chief of naval operations. Congress eventually enacted legislation ensuring that the marine corps remained a separate service, and Truman did not object.

The most controversial dissent came from five-star army general Douglas MacArthur, who led the United Nations Command at the beginning of the Korean War. The arrogance of the supercilious MacArthur grated on President Truman. MacArthur persisted in advocating publicly that the war in Korea be expanded to include ground assaults into southern China, an escalation Truman steadfastly opposed. When MacArthur ignored White House requests that he desist, an irate President Truman decided to fire him. The Joint Chiefs of Staff agreed, albeit reluctantly, with their commander in chief's decision, because MacArthur was implicitly disobeying the constitutional imperative of civilian control. The Joint Chiefs, however, believed his words were imperious rather than deliberately insubordinate, an action that can result in a court-martial.

During Kennedy's brief presidency, there were two instances of dissent. The first occurred during the Bay of Pigs invasion. To overthrow the Castro regime in Cuba, the CIA had recruited and semi-trained a force of several thousand Cuban émigrés. The plan was to land them on an isolated beachhead. From there, they could consolidate, link up with anti-Castro guerrillas, and initiate a countrywide uprising. The actual landing, however, was a disaster. The fledgling Cuban air force, not destroyed preinvasion, attacked the unarmed transport ships. The critical planning assumption was that US Navy fighter and attack planes would protect the landing. At the last minute, President Kennedy canceled all air support. It was a spur-of-the-moment decision, done with no consultation. The colonel assigned by the Pentagon to coordinate the air support of the landing was caught utterly by surprise. Over the next day, as the Cuban landing force was defeated, he mulled resigning in protest, but he did not. An embarrassed and furious Kennedy blamed the CIA for the whole Bay

of Pigs fiasco. There was no acknowledgment that US air support most likely would have resulted in a successful landing, at least for the initial month or so.

The second matter of dissent followed after the Cuban Missile Crisis in 1962. Secretary of Defense Robert McNamara privately told President Kennedy that the chief of naval operations, Admiral George Anderson, had been insubordinate during the crisis. McNamara resented that during the crisis the CNO had told him naval operations weren't his business. Acceding to his secretary of defense, the president did not, as was standard, offer the CNO a second two-year appointment.

In sum, in terms of immediate (1918–65) historical context prior to Vietnam, military dissent about the objectives or the conduct of a war occurred only in the person of General MacArthur. Even then, it's not clear whether he was actually advocating an actual war strategy of attacking inside China, or whether he was, as the Joint Chiefs of Staff at the time chose to believe, merely ruminating.

In the next three wars (Vietnam, Iraq, and Afghanistan), however, America met with failure. Was there military dissent about either a flawed military strategy or impossible war objectives?

Broadly speaking, leadership in war comes from three hubs. The first hub is the policy makers, including the president as commander in chief and the chairman of the Joint Chiefs of Staff as his military adviser, plus the field commander in the geographic theater of war, the CIA, the State Department, and the secretary of defense, all of whom give input that is heeded or ignored, depending on the personality of the president. The second hub is the culture and popular mood of our country, as reflected by congressional votes and the slant of the mainstream press. The press does not report "just the facts"; rather, it presents a point of view by selecting which facts to focus on. The popular mood is the ultimate fulcrum of political power, because the policy hub can't fight a war without resources from Congress. The third hub consists of the generals and admirals who design the operational strategy that determines how our troops will fight. As our recent wars illustrate, however, often the operational strategy is undercut or severely altered by the policy hub, even though all parties seemed in agreement when the war was initiated.

VIETNAM

In 1965, when President Lyndon Johnson wrestled with sending US forces into South Vietnam, he called the chairman of the Joint Chiefs of Staff and the four service chiefs into the Oval Office. They laid out a robust war plan, including sustained bombing of North Vietnam and mining its harbors to prevent the Soviet and Chinese shipment of war materials. In response, Johnson exploded in anger, swearing and cursing at the generals, insulting their character and intelligence, chasing them from his office. Taking counsel of his fears, he was terrified that the strategy advocated by the Joint Chiefs would provoke China into sending hundreds of thousands of soldiers a thousand miles through rice paddies and jungles to fight in South Vietnam.

So was the die cast. The president and a small civilian coterie—particularly a supine yet arrogant Secretary of Defense Robert McNamara—would determine military strategy, not the generals. For the next four years, Johnson's inner circle made incremental war decisions based on doing the minimum, shutting out Congress and misleading the public. Their guiding idea was that erratic demonstrations of American power would convince North Vietnam to desist.

The Joint Chiefs believed that a half-million American troops, heavy bombing across North Vietnam, and ground incursions into the North were necessary. But after Johnson tongue-lashed and scorned them, not one dissented or resigned. Instead, they backed a commander in Vietnam, Army General William Westmoreland, who waged a senseless war of attrition, sending American battalions in the jungle to slug it out with tough North Vietnamese soldiers, whose government was willing to sacrifice a million of them to seize the South.

In Northern I Corps, the marines went in a different direction, patrolling to push the Viet Cong insurgents out of the villages. Their goal was to prevail in a classic guerrilla war by cutting off the insurgents from the people. Success was stymied, however, when tens of thousands of North Vietnamese soldiers poured south. What started as a guerrilla war in mid-1965 had escalated into a full-fledged conventional invasion a year later. Ordered not to outflank the enemy by forays into Laos or North Vietnam and kept to a narrow front, for the next two years the marines fought defensive battles that made no strategic sense and often were poorly executed.

In terms of doctrine, the marines profoundly disagreed with General Westmoreland's operational concept of "search & destroy." The marines believed the North Vietnamese were willing to lose five to ten times more soldiers, while continuing to attack until the American popular will wilted. But ironically, the marines had no choice except to do the same as the North Vietnamese persisted in attacking.

There were only two ways out for the American military. The first was a MacArthur-like public dissent aimed at forcing the Johnson policy hub to alter its restrictions on the military operational strategy, allowing sustained bombing of the North and flanking operations on the ground and from the sea. While many generals believed in that course of action, none resigned or created a furor by publicly dissenting. One partial reason was that the press was mocking, rather than praising General Westmoreland. This meant that no general had the public status to challenge the Johnson clique.

Between 1965 and 1967, Congress and the public were basically supportive of the war and the press fixated more on the gore of battle than the lack of a coherent strategy. That changed in February of 1968, however, when during the Tet holidays the North Vietnamese Army (NVA) and the southern Viet Cong guerrillas launched a full-scale assault on the cities, expecting the residents to rise up in support. Instead, the exposed insurgent (Viet Cong) infrastructure was shattered and the NVA regulars were decimated.

But the American press had portrayed the 1968 assault on the cities as definitive proof that the war could not be won, while extolling student protests against the war and the draft. President Johnson, thoroughly beaten and exhausted by his own political machinations, did not run for reelection.

The advent of Richard Nixon's presidential administration opened the second way out of Vietnam for the American military. This required standing up a South Vietnamese army that could defend against both the North Vietnamese regulars and the clandestine Viet Cong guerrilla movement. Between 1968 and 1970, American tactics improved dramatically and the NVA was driven deep into the jungles. When the American military withdrew in 1972, civilian traffic was able to move unmolested throughout most of the populated areas near the coast. At the same time, tens of thousands of North Vietnamese soldiers waited and watched from the highlands and jungles of South Vietnam.

President Thieu of South Vietnam was furious when Nixon forced him to agree to a flimsy truce that allowed the North Vietnamese to remain hiding in the South. No American general, however, dissented to the Nixon policy of total withdrawal of US troops. After President Richard Nixon resigned in disgrace in 1974, the executive branch conceded to Congress total control of decision making about Vietnam. Nixon's promises to provide South Vietnam with fulsome aid and to bomb any North Vietnamese offensive counted for nothing. The Democratic Senate and House passed legislation prohibiting US bombing anywhere in Southeast Asia, regardless of provocation. Military aid to South Vietnam was slashed to a pittance, while massive Soviet and Chinese armaments rebuilt the NVA. In 1975, the NVA seized South Vietnam.

IRAQ

On September 11, 2001, two commercial aircraft crashed into and destroyed the Twin Towers, killing three thousand civilians. Islamist terrorists had plotted the attack from Afghanistan. America swiftly counterattacked into Afghanistan, and the enemy scattered. As the fighting subsided in 2002, President George W. Bush changed the mission from destroying al-Qaeda to transforming Afghanistan into a democracy. At the same time, he pivoted the policy attention of the White House and the resources of the military toward Iraq.

Bush believed the nexus of evil in the Middle East was Saddam Hussein, the tyrant controlling Iraq. With Afghanistan seemingly under control, Bush decided to remove Saddam before he transferred weapons of mass destruction—chemicals and eventually nuclear—to terrorists. Presented evidence of weapons of mass destruction that later proved to be accidentally in error, in early 2003 Congress and the United Nations approved the invasion of Iraq. But after no weapons of mass destruction were found, Bush made the critical decision to stay in Iraq for the long term.

He declared America was duty bound to remain in order to transform Iraq into a vibrant democracy. One of the first acts of our policy leaders then was to unwisely disband the Iraqi army. The American military took its place, declaring that our soldiers and marines were nation builders as well as warriors. Although this was a vast expanse of the military's mission and included tasks for which the US Army and Marines were not trained, our generals endorsed nation building without internal debate or dissent. This was the most critical decision of the war by our generals. It changed the roles of our soldiers into that of civilian administrators, police, contractors, and ombudsmen.

Our policy makers then abetted the emergence of a central government controlled by sly, vengeful Shiite politicians intent on disenfranchising the Sunni minority that had persecuted the majority Shiites for decades. Our policy makers then bumbled badly in 2004, handing over the key Sunni city of Fallujah to the al-Qaeda in Iraq (AQI) terrorist network. Internally, several American generals did strongly dissent from withdrawing our troops from Fallujah, but to no avail. As a direct result of our military retreat, AQI grew in strength, bombing Shiite mosques and igniting a civil war, while assassinating Sunni sheiks and posing as the protectors of the Sunni people.

What followed were two years of chaos. As in Vietnam, among our generals there was internal dissent. The army concluded that American soldiers patrolling the streets were an antibody rejected by Shiites and Sunnis alike. The marines insisted on intense patrolling to hunt down the elusive AQI terrorists and to win over the Sunni tribes. In this, they were unsuccessful and frustrated until November of 2006. At that time, US soldiers in Anbar Province in western Iraq rescued a powerful sheik about to be murdered by AQI. Once rescued, the sheik turned against AQI. He rallied his tribe, threw in with the Americans, and urged all other Sunni sheiks to do likewise.

By the end of 2006, the Sunni tribes across western Iraq had allied with the marines and were pointing out the terrorists who had been hiding in plain sight. AQI was forced to flee.

Despite severe congressional opposition, in early 2007 President Bush surged an additional twenty-five thousand troops into Iraq. General David Petraeus assumed overall command in Baghdad and paid for the creation of Sunni neighborhood militias across central and northern Iraq. This both drove out the Sunni terrorists and prevented Shiite militias from moving into Sunni neighborhoods. By 2010, Iraq was relatively stable, with a residual force of several thousand American soldiers on bases inside Baghdad and key provinces, acting both as ombudsmen settling Sunni-Shiite political disputes and as watchdogs guarding against the excesses of the Shiite-controlled central government.

However, in late 2011, President Obama and Vice President Biden pulled all US troops out of the country. Our senior generals and senior diplomats respectfully but publicly and forcefully dissented, testifying that they believed a total withdrawal was premature and that Iraq would fracture along sectarian lines. Within two years, that happened and al-Qaeda, reconstituted as the Islamic State of Iraq and Syria, or ISIS, seized the western cities of Ramadi and Fallujah and threatened to storm into Baghdad. Obama had to hastily deploy

US combat power and advisers that fought until 2018, when they finally crushed ISIS as a fighting force. By that time, President Trump had been elected. Where President Bush was evangelical in viewing America's global role, President Obama suggested that America historically had acted as a colonial overlord whose power had to be curtailed. These two separate fonts of strategic thinking were rejected by President Trump, whose global view was based on transactions rather than values or interpretations of history. He defined foreign policy as a matter of quid pro quos in place of steadfast alliances or enduring principles. In his view, the American mission in Iraq was over. As Obama had done, so too did Trump pull out our troops, again over the strong but respectful dissent of our generals.

Once our troops were gone, Iran increased its support for the Shiite militias it controlled and orchestrated missile attacks to harass our few bases. By 2022, Iraq was a country wracked by corruption and strife. Whether it emerged as a truly sovereign nation or as a satrap of Iran was not predictable. In either event, two decades after the American-led, UN-backed invasion, Iraq could not be defined as a stable, prosperous democracy.

This was not due to any shift in American popular opinion, which played a small role as the Iraq War waxed and waned over the past two decades. With no draft, there was no student protest movement. In huge distinction from Vietnam, the press and those who disapproved of the war supported the troops.

The failure in Iraq rested squarely with three presidents. The rationale for the war and the decision to "nation-build" was made by President Bush. The military too quickly adopted nation building as its mission. Our generals quietly assessed that the State Department and the Agency for International Development were not properly manned, capable, or willing to undertake massive nation building. While this was true, the military stretched its "can-do" spirit too far.

President Bush initiated a war that he could not conclude on his watch. The military failed to make that clear to him. The generals endorsed rather than dissented when presented with the nation-building mission. That was a close call: what choice did they really have? They could not stand to one side, and, despite faltering badly in 2005–6, by late 2006 the Sunni tribes had come over to the side of the American military. Our military had succeeded in holding the country together and keeping at bay the malign influences of the Sunni terrorists and the Iranian-backed radical Shiite militias.

However, then two successive presidents—Obama and Trump—deliberately deconstructed the gains made. In both cases, our generals did clearly and respectfully dissent when both Presidents Obama and Trump pulled out our troops.

AFGHANISTAN

This is a markedly different story. Al-Qaeda struck the Twin Towers on 9/11. By November, al-Qaeda's top leaders and core fighters inside Afghanistan had fallen back into the snow-packed mountains called Tora Bora. Marine Brigadier General Jim Mattis had landed in southern Afghanistan with three thousand marines and Special Forces. He proposed to our top command inserting his troops on the dozen passes out of Tora Bora, thus trapping al-Qaeda inside and then destroying them. For reasons never explained, he was refused by our top military command. A senior CIA officer asked President Bush to reverse the decision, but he demurred. Years later, Donald Rumsfeld, the secretary of defense in 2001, opined that the president did not want to interfere in the military chain of command. That deference, combined with the terrible decision of the military top command, allowed al-Qaeda to escape into the sanctuary of Pakistan, a duplicitous state supportive of Islamist fundamentalism.

By the beginning of 2002, inside Afghanistan the Islamist government called the Taliban and the Islamist terrorists called al-Qaeda were in disarray and in hiding. The policy hub, strongly led by the president, then decided America was obliged to transform a confederation of fractious tribes into a self-sustained democracy. That was a pivotal, critical decision made without serious dissent from our intelligence and military communities.

Over the next seven years, security deteriorated along the entire eastern portion of the country. Pakistan, congenitally duplicitous, was providing the Taliban with a sanctuary and material aid, while in Kabul an erratic, untrustworthy President Karzai railed against American bombing and kept quiet about the Taliban. The country lacked a sense of nationalism and there was no draft. Afghan soldiers from northern Tajik tribes were sent into the eastern and southeastern Pashtun provinces to fight Pashtun Taliban. For years, American and allied soldiers patrolled through disputed hamlets along the eastern half of the country—with a porous 1,500-mile-long border with Pakistan—controlling only the ground they stood upon. As soon as they left, the Taliban would pop back up.

Our top generals believed that with more troops, American soldiers could win the allegiance of the Pashtun tribe (nine million strong) as they had the Sunni tribes in Iraq in 2006–7. In late 2009, President Obama reluctantly agreed to surge an additional thirty thousand troops into Afghanistan. At the same time, both he and Vice President Joe Biden made clear their distrust of the generals. Nevertheless, Obama approved relieving the top American general in Afghanistan and replacing him with a general dedicated to an unproven counterinsurgency strategy called the "oil spot." The concept called for American troops to clear the Taliban from the rural villages and hold those villages until relieved by Afghan soldiers, who in turn would build trust among the elders by doling out US money and projects. This bubble of security would spread outward like an oil spot.

From a battalion commander with seven hundred troops down to a platoon commander with fifty, it was clear to those on the ground that the oil spot was fantastical. Practically, our troops patrolled by walking about three miles a day in heavy gear in formations of fifteen to twenty men. They did not speak Pashto and at best would glumly sip tea for an hour with dispassionate elders in some unnamed hamlet. They would exchange rifle fire with Taliban hiding on the hillsides and leave, braving the IEDs (improvised explosive devices) sure to be encountered on the return trip. Our grunts did not believe

Afghan soldiers would ever hold those isolated villages, separated by steep mountain ridges or hundreds of acres of corn and poppy called the "Green Zone."

This was frustrating to our warriors. Our military technology had outstripped the rest of the world. Most telling was our leap forward in air-to-ground surveillance, detection, and destruction. Militaries cannot move or be supplied without vehicles. Every internal engine, every artillery tube that fires, indeed every human face emits heat that shines like a spotlight and can be detected by American systems. Use any computer or cell phone, walk outdoors, drive down a road— and you can be tracked.

Yet despite these extraordinary systems, our troops did not quash the Taliban. Why? Simple: the enemy adapted. He took off his uniform and used our morality as jiujitsu to overcome our technological advantages. The goal was to win over the people. Thus rules of engagement were designed to place severe limits on the use of indirect (mortars, artillery, rockets, or bombs) firepower. Even one civilian casualty caused bitter complaints, although the Taliban were responsible for three out of four killed or wounded.

By hiding without fear of betrayal among the people, the Taliban were safe from our firepower. They came together in small groups, choosing when and where to initiate contact against our patrols. It became common for a platoon commander to say, "My mission is to get every one of my men back home in one piece." Why risk your men when no one could tell you what defined victory?

Yet dissent did not bubble up from the battlefields, forcing the generals to review and change the counterinsurgency/nation-building doctrine. There was a clog in the military reporting system. Over two decades, an uninterrupted succession of American commanding generals talked of progress and foresaw success. Lieutenant colonels who commanded battalions morphed into advocates of the oil spot clear-hold-build concept when they were promoted to higher ranks.

Nine American generals held the top command in Afghanistan. Yet throughout their combined tenures, the counterinsurgency doctrine of clear-hold-build and win tribal fealty toward the Kabul government remained unchallenged among our general officers. There was no dissent. This glaring gap separating the assessments of the grunts from those of the generals demands explanation. Throughout the deteriorating course of the war, the press and Congress remained largely supportive. The popular mood gradually shifted toward war-weariness, not toward political opposition.

Beginning in 2014, the American/allied campaign strategy did focus on training the Afghan army. But "the right stuff" wasn't there. Leadership and morale on the government side remained spotty, while tribal allegiances to tribes remained high. American commanders adhered to "soft power" enticements, such as construction money, to woo over the Pashtun tribes. It didn't work. Year after year, the rural areas of southern and eastern Afghanistan fell under the control of the Taliban. Our generals kept saying, "This war can't be won by killing," while the Taliban kept moving forward by killing American and Afghan soldiers.

At the same time, our senior generals were wary of the consequences of losing in the fashion that had befallen us in South Vietnam. The global image and the reputation of America were not intangibles to be blithely dismissed. While by 2017 the US troop level had fallen well below twenty thousand, when NATO forces and contractors were added, there was still a potent fighting force in the country. Given the proper mentorship and aerial fire support, many Afghan units were fighting with moderate success. The net result pointed toward a stalemate, with the Kabul government holding the cities and the Taliban controlling the countryside. This was not the robust democracy President Bush had envisioned, but it was not a public defeat.

When President Trump became president, he faced a secretary of defense and chairman of the Joint Chiefs of Staff who were firm in recommending the indefinite maintenance of a small force (around ten thousand troops) to advise and train Afghan units and reassure them by our continued presence, plus steady bombing. Ignoring that advice, in 2019 President Trump negotiated ambiguous terms with the Taliban. He indicated he intended to pull out all US troops, but only after he was reelected. He lost the election.

In April of 2021, however, President Biden did order a total pull-out. It is not clear if our senior military internally registered strong dissent. Publicly, there was no dissent. And once they grasped that they were going to be left on their own, the Afghan forces collapsed. The result was a disaster, with panic prevailing at the Kabul airport in August as hundreds of thousands tried to flee. It was a humiliating ending, tragic for the women of Afghanistan and for the basic principle of freedom. As in the case of Vietnam, the unresolved question was whether the Kabul government would have survived had the United States left a small residual force.

What was not in dispute, however, was that the military strategy of the oil spot clear-hold-build was fatally flawed. Yet it had remained the prevailing doctrine for a dozen years, despite the widespread belief among the grunts that it could not succeed. That lack of dissent among the top military ranks was a deep flaw.

Of more concern than the issue of military dissent was the role of the policy hub (the senior officials at the CIA, State Department, and Pentagon) clustered around and directed by the White House. Our Founding Fathers intended to limit the power of the executive branch, and Thomas Jefferson warned about the "idolatry of royalty." But over the past seventy years, the executive branch has accumulated more power than wisdom. In all three wars, the policy hub—not the military and not Congress—was primarily responsible for the failure. In not one case did the president who initiated the hostilities conclude them before he left office. If those three successive failures told us anything, it was that the policy hub emanating from the White House had grown too confident of its own quixotic infallibility, unchallenged by a divisive Congress that was supine in matters of war.

UKRAINE

Against that background, in 2022 we faced the Russian invasion of Ukraine. Given the unifying effect of waging a war for survival between 1941 and 1945, our culture believed in a genuine division between good and evil. We as a nation in World War II did support Stalin against the greater immediate evil manifested in Hitler's regime. But the American body politic agreed with Churchill's condemnation of the totalitarian Soviet Union as requiring an Iron Curtain to block its move toward the west.

America's cultural ethos, however, fractured badly during the Vietnam War. After that, we seemed to have shrugged off leaving Iraq in a perilous state and consigning Afghanistan in 2021 to a ninth-century Islamist autocracy. Unlike Vietnam, Iraq, and Afghanistan, however, the destruction of Ukraine and the valiant defense of its people struck home. How the Ukraine war plays out will be more important to the security of the West than were the previous three wars of Vietnam, Iraq, and Afghanistan. With the all-out invasion of Ukraine, Russia mocked the notion of secure national borders or an international order based on mutual agreement to rules-based behavior. Russia under Putin has challenged the bedrock principles that held NATO and the West together.

And the thesis central to this essay has again been confirmed. As was true in the cases of Vietnam, Iraq, and Afghanistan, the White House, not Congress, has determined the response in Ukraine. With supreme self-confidence, Joseph Biden as vice president had supported our withdrawal from Iraq in 2012 and as president in 2021 had ordered our chaotic pullout from Afghanistan. As regards Ukraine, he has refused to set an objective for American involvement in supplying arms or otherwise supporting Ukraine. He has not said whether the goal is Ukraine free of Russian occupying forces.

Before the invasion, Biden believed his threat of economic sanctions would deter Putin. When his threat failed and Putin did invade, Biden contradicted himself, claiming sanctions cannot deter an aggressor. In the opening days of the war, it was hard not to conclude that the Biden White House had expected a swift Russian victory, with the West indulging in rhetorical outrage while returning to postwar trade and relationships. But Ukraine did not crack.

In 1940, President Roosevelt, faced with a reluctant public and Congress, employed bold stratagems to deliver military aid to beleaguered England. However, President Biden, faced with a pro-military aid public and Congress, resisted giving heavy arms to Ukraine.

"What is NATO doing? Is it being run by Russia?" a frustrated President Zelensky asked. "Ukraine needs tanks, planes, antiaircraft-defense and anti-ship missiles. Our allies have these resources, but they prefer to allow them collect dust in their warehouses."

In early March, Poland had offered thirty MiG-29s. Secretary of State Antony Blinken gave the request a "green light." In response, Putin offhandedly threatened nuclear retaliation. President Biden then vetoed the MiG-29s. His timidity is cast into sharp release when compared to Russia during the Vietnam War. In 1966, America's nuclear superiority was overwhelming: the United States possessed 5,000 nuclear warheads versus 550 in the Soviet Union. The Soviets felt the only stable nuclear situation was one in which one side had clear superiority over the other. They knew they were on the losing side in any escalation, but they were unfazed.

The Russians supplied the heavy arms to kill thousands of American soldiers and secure a victory for North Vietnam. They provided hundreds of MiGs to engage our jets in air-to-air combat; Biden vetoed the transfer of thirty MiGs to Ukraine. About three thousand Soviet trainers were stationed inside North Vietnam. Bizarrely, our military has bragged that it is training no Ukrainians, not even inside Poland. Russia provided North Vietnam with two thousand tanks and seven thousand artillery pieces. Our troops on muddy outposts like Khe Sanh and Con Thien were shelled day and night by Russian artillery. President Biden resisted transferring any tanks or artillery to Ukrainians until the second month of the war.

Why? Following Putin's casual reference to nuclear weapons, President Biden's hesitation to robustly aid Ukraine set a terrible precedent. It provided a persuasive rationale for many nations to acquire nuclear weapons. An aggressor with nukes could invade another country without fear of a conventional counteroffensive against his homeland. Conversely, a country armed with nuclear weapons was less apt to be invaded in the first place. Either way, President Biden had reduced belief in any American security guarantee or umbrella deflecting any nuclear attack.

While members of Congress criticized Biden's halfway measures, no active-duty general testifying before Congress registered a murmur of disagreement or dissent. Yet the experience of any general had surely set off alarm bells about the inadequacy of military support being provided to Ukraine.

Although the war is ongoing, it is not too early or premature to address its effect in terms of American interests. Two alternative futures have emerged. The first is a postwar return to the status quo ante. This end state has been clearly set forth by Secretary of State Blinken. "This is already a strategic defeat for Vladimir Putin," Blinken said in April of 2022. "If it [Ukraine] concludes that it can bring this war to an end . . . and that requires the lifting of sanctions, we're going to look at that. The purpose of the sanctions is not to be there indefinitely. It's to change Russia's conduct. And if, as a result of negotiations . . . we achieve that, then at some point the sanctions will go away."

In this alternative, the Biden administration and NATO propose that sanctions will cease as soon as Russia changes its conduct, to include pledging not again to invade Ukraine or any other country. Of course Putin will offer that guarantee in triplicate. Blinken has guaranteed Putin that he cannot lose. Once Putin is confident that "sanctions will go away," he is certain to agree to a cease-fire. As in any negotiation, there will be some clauses he can display as a victory trophy to the Russian people. With sanctions lifted, money will flow in to replenish his military treasure chest. Once rearmed, a smoldering Putin will be empowered to lash out again, choosing both the time and venue. Like Britain's Prime Minister Neville Chamberlain in 1938, Secretary of State Blinken is pursuing "peace in our time," camouflage for a humiliating defeat for the West.

Having called Putin a war criminal and butcher, Biden will be forced to consider the second alternative future: expelling Russia from the ranks of nations that believe in secure borders and the dignity of man. The stakes extend far beyond Ukraine. Russia must be isolated and excluded. This war isn't about one human being. Sanctions must remain imposed for a decade or more to punish Russian aggression and restrict its military resurgence. This means cutting off Russian oil and gas exports to the West, most severely affecting Germany and Italy. It is doubtful he or the rulers in Germany will go that route.

If they did, then regardless of any negotiation about Ukraine, a second Cold War would begin to keep Russia penned in. It would persist for decades to come. While the first Cold War persisted for four decades, it did not impede the growth of wealth and freedom in the West. Like Stalin, Mao, and Castro, there's a good chance Putin will die many years from now while still in power. Regardless of when he leaves the scene, Russian soldiers murdering civilians revealed a brutal martial culture built on a totalitarian, effective chain command. That culture must be enchained until it is excised. Russia can be granted no surcease. Resolve is the long-term test facing the West. China is the larger and more dangerous long-term threat. If the Russian invasion ends with Russian troops occupying a large portion of Ukraine and controlling the Black Sea, then the odds increase of China's belligerence.

The credibility of the West depends on which alternative future President Biden chooses. Hopefully, our generals who safeguard our security will forcefully and respectfully register their agreement or dissent about the objectives of the new Cold War.

EPILOGUE: CIVILIAN–MILITARY RELATIONS IN THE NEWS

Victor Davis Hanson

The essays in this book are not just historical studies. In the spirit of the Hoover Institution's Role of Military History in Contemporary Conflict Working Group, they are designed to offer help in assessing and understanding contemporary military conflict and violence at home and abroad. Perhaps rarely in recent memory have contemporary Americans needed such historic guidance about the interconnected roles of their military, their elected officials, and the citizenry at large.

During the four years of the Donald Trump administration, complaints arose that the sometimes-fragile American civilian–military relationship was radically endangered—an institution that has always been defined in a variety of ways. Civilians exercise complete control over the military, given that our Constitution and Founders worried far more about the abuse of political power by generals and admirals than about incompetent politicians without military expertise interfering in matters of war making, strategy, and tactics. Americans have the right to speak freely and protest in a lawful manner without fear of a military crackdown or coup, given that their troops are citizens first and soldiers second. In recent years, however, critics have charged that these foundational norms are now under rare assault.

Ironically, President Trump was initially faulted for appearing overly accommodating to the military by nominating too many retired four-star generals to his cabinet—Generals John Kelly (director of homeland security), Michael Flynn (national security advisor), James Mattis (secretary of defense), and H. R. McMaster (national security advisor). As a real estate magnate, Trump often defended his military nominees by citing his World War II heroes Generals George S. Patton and Douglas MacArthur as models of the sorts of dynamic, can-do men of action whom the military produced and he felt he needed in government. In the case of the recently retired General Mattis, Trump requested and received a rare congressional waiver of the required seven-year cooling-off period between military service and appointment as secretary. Trump markedly raised the defense budget after years of budgetary cuts and deferred to the Pentagon on matters of major defense procurements.

Yet Trump's romance with the military and its high-ranking retired generals—again, severely criticized by the Left—proved short lived indeed. Just days after his inauguration, former Pentagon legal counselor Rosa Brooks published a startling January 30, 2017, article in *Foreign Policy*, raising the issue of a necessary coup to remove the newly inaugurated Trump:

> Trump's first week as president has made it all too clear: Yes, he is as crazy as everyone feared. . . . A possibility [for removing Trump from office] is one that until recently I would have said was unthinkable in the United States of America: a military coup, or at least a refusal by military leaders to obey certain orders.

Indeed, within three years of their nominations or appointments *all* four generals had either resigned or been fired by Trump, and two upon release had become fierce public critics of the president. As the 2020 elections approached, several prominent retired four-star officers went public in their denunciations of Trump for supposedly displaying Nazi, Mussolinian, or Hitlerian tendencies. Such disparagements of their commander in chief were all likely violations of 10 U.S.C. Section 888, Article 88, of the Uniform Code of Military Justice that applies equally to retired generals and admirals and forbids officers from disparaging their commander in chief.

More controversially, chairman of the Joint Chiefs of Staff Mark Milley, appointed by Trump to the chief military advisory role in the government, later confirmed journalistic accounts that on his own initiative he had privately contacted his Chinese counterpart, General Li Zuocheng, of the People's Liberation Army. Milley sought to reassure the Chinese military that should his own supposedly unsteady commander in chief Trump indicate any willingness to resort to using nuclear weapons during a crisis, Milley on his own initiative would then warn the Chinese military in advance that he, General Mark Milley, would do his best to override any such mercurial presidential order.

Bipartisan observers noted that there was no evidence that the often-bombastic Trump, a fierce critic of prior optional American ground wars in the Middle East, had shown any inclination to prompt a crisis, much less ignite one with nuclear weapons. They demanded that Milley show evidence of any such Strangelovian inclinations on the part of the president. And they noted in addition that Milley had likely further exceeded his own advisory authority in reportedly ordering theater commanders to channel any presidential orders and protocols considering the use of nuclear weapons through his own person.

Trump critic Lieutenant Colonel Alexander Vindman, a key prosecutorial witness in an earlier successful impeachment of Trump, at the time blasted Milley in a public tweet of September 14, 2021, and called for his resignation on grounds that he had "usurped civilian authority, broke Chain of Command, and violated the sacrosanct principle of civilian control over the military."

By election time, the polarization between President Trump and the active and retired officer corps was complete. Democratic nominee Joe Biden was loudly reassuring the country that if incumbent president Donald Trump were to steal the November 2020 election—as judged by Biden himself—then he had complete confidence that esteemed "military leaders" and "the rank and file" would "escort him from the White House with great dispatch."

Amid this civilian–military conundrum, Trump supporters claimed that the military, in the manner of the top echelon of a now politicized FBI and CIA, was dangerously freelancing into political territory far outside its statutory purviews. They further charged that high-ranking officers had overreached because they feared the outsider Trump's unorthodox political agendas and behavior—to the point that they were willing to violate both federal statutes and constitutional guardrails designed to ensure that such a supposed menace to the republic was neutralized. In essence, they were on the brink of a veritable *Seven Days in May* coup of the sort raised for consideration in 2017 by Rosa Brooks.

Trump opponents praised the new activist role of the military, given that they believed Trump truly was a threat to constitutional norms. The Left now warmed to the Pentagon as it praised the supposed preemptive vigilance from members of the military establishment. As guardians of the Constitution sworn to defend it against perceived enemies foreign and domestic, generals, retired and active, were rising to the occasion against existential threats like President Trump.

In response, conservative retired generals began blasting the new political activism of their colleagues, while defenders of outspoken retired generals retorted that Trump himself was a sui generis threat to the Constitution. Few noted that generals of any political persuasion should not be partisans in the political arena, called upon by politicians to adjudicate matters better left to the courts and Congress. Polls apparently agreed, as the military suffered a historic decline in public confidence that became even worse during the subsequent Biden administration. According to a survey conducted by the Ronald Reagan Presidential Foundation and Institute in fall 2021, following such public acrimony and the flight from Afghanistan, only 45 percent of the American people polled reported a "great deal of confidence" in their military—a drop from 70 percent as measured by the same survey in 2018.

Both sides apparently agreed that the military had now assumed a new activist role in politics, whether redoubtable or salutary—but one clearly abhorrent to the public. Few knew whether such military interventionism into civilian affairs marked a one-off, isolated event justified by the singular presidency of Donald Trump or presaged a new frightening assumption of influence by top generals, active and retired.

On the one hand, would four or more generals now be routinely nominated to a presidential cabinet? On the other, would generals freelance and call up their enemy counterparts to apprise them of what they thought was unpredictable presidential behavior? And would retired officers routinely and publicly blast their current commander in chief as reminiscent of some of the most reprehensible dictators in modern history?

Yet military opposition to an elected government has not been the only sort of tension in civilian–military affairs during recent years. In summer 2020, 120 days of near-constant riots, spearheaded by Antifa and Black Lives Matter protestors, resulted in over $1 billion in property damage, more than 35 deaths, injury to some 1,500 police officers, and more than 14,000 arrests. Across the country, public buildings, including police precincts and a federal courthouse, were torched.

At one point on May 31, 2020, protestors nearly stormed the White House grounds, prompting the Secret Service to remove Trump to a secure location. Meanwhile, in blue states such as Oregon, Minnesota, and Washington, local and state law enforcement did not promptly quell their own violence—at least not as quickly as some in Washington demanded—the laxity perceived as given to the political nature of the protests, the personal unpopularity of Trump, and a looming divisive presidential election. The growing violence in the streets prompted President Trump, in the fashion of a dozen prior presidents, to consider calling in federal troops to quell the disturbances. Yet there was now an important qualifier: this time around, any arrival of federalized troops would likely be *against*, not in accordance with, the wishes of governors and mayors.

Almost immediately, former high-ranking officers blasted Trump's consideration of such federal deployments. The omnipresent Joint

Chiefs chairman General Mark Milley reassured the press that he should not have done a photo op with his commander in chief at the scene of the burned historic St. John's Episcopal Church near the White House. He apologized to the country for supposedly being used as political prop to greenlight Trump's possible orders to call out the military.

The drama was not over. Seven months later, on January 6, following the controversial election of 2020 and the defeat of Trump, pro-Trump rioters unlawfully entered the Capitol and ransacked the House chambers, prompting mass arrests. Five died—one Capitol officer, of natural causes, and four Trump supporters, at least one violently: an unarmed female veteran was lethally shot by a Capitol Police officer as she climbed unlawfully through a window into the Capitol chambers. Public and media outrage arose over not just Trump's failure to stop the demonstration but also his earlier encouragement of a massive turnout that logically might have led to such violence.

As a result, the US military was now called into action. It oversaw the deployment of more than 25,000 National Guard troops stationed throughout Washington, DC, in the largest array of armed forces in the nation's capital since the Civil War—but this time with no enemy army anywhere on the horizon. Trump was subsequently impeached in the House for allegedly encouraging the riot or failing as commander in chief to stop it. Although acquitted in the Senate, Trump became the first president in US history to be impeached both twice and while out of office as a private citizen.

As thousands of troops erected barricades and strung barbed wire, the Right that had often called for troops to quell the riot and arson of 2020 now deplored the allegedly political use of US military troops in a manner far beyond any reasonable civilian threat. Similarly, the Left that had fiercely attacked Trump for even considering sending the army or National Guard into riot-torn major US cities during the summer 2020 now applauded the militarization of the national capital as a necessary deterrent against any further right-wing demonstrations.

Had fragile military–political relations hit rock bottom in dangerous fashion?

Had civilian protests in the streets of America been encouraged by
the failure to deploy military troops, or, contrarily, was the military
improperly garrisoning the Capitol for abjectly political purposes?

Again, the only common denominator was that both Left and
Right would agree that an activist military was now involved in civilian decision making in a manner that seemed unprecedented in a
constitutional state.

So, were the years 2017 to 2020 unprecedented?

The evidence of this volume may suggest no. These chapters chronicle a historically tense relationship between the army and the state and
the outbreak of dissent within the military during times of crisis and
war across time and space. In these examples widely ranging over some
2,500 years of Western constitutional governments, there emerges
from these historical studies a consensus that such tripartite tensions
between civilians, elected officials, and soldiers are not so rare at all.
They may be often dangerous and violent but also seem innate and
pose frequent challenges to democratic and republican government.

For all the turmoil of recent years, the House and the Senate
certainly never voted to execute their generals in the manner of
the Athenian assembly after the victory at Arginusae. Draft rioting
during the Civil War far exceeded in intensity and destruction the
violence of 2020. Copperhead state governors and public officials
during the Civil War often openly defied the Lincoln administration, which occasionally resorted to the suspension of habeas corpus. And if generals played too prominent a role in recent politics,
they certainly did not turn on the Union and help form a separate
Confederacy. Fired Union general George McClellan came out of
retirement in 1864 to challenge the incumbent president Lincoln on
the grounds that the president's military incompetence demanded
a negotiated settlement, not a Union victory, to end the Civil War.

General Mark Milley and a variety of retired generals may have
variously exceeded their statuary authority by either freelancing in
foreign policy or crudely deriding their president. But such activism

pales in comparison to General Douglas MacArthur's open and public defiance of President Harry Truman at critical junctures during the Korean War.

As we have seen in this volume, there were several occasions—during the Korean conflict, the Vietnam War, the bitter procurement interservice rivalries during the Cold War, and the more recent wars in Afghanistan and Iraq—when presidential decisions were clearly mistaken, when they risked losing wars critical to national security and prompted military officers to circumvent or occasionally openly defy presidential edicts. On the other hand, when high-ranking officers did not question clearly flawed civilian decision making, properly through the chain of command—as the recent catastrophe in Afghanistan might suggest—a president's calamitous errors have cost lives and eroded national deterrence.

In sum, each generation properly worries about existential dangers to the republic when thousands in the street violently protest political decisions or war policies, or when officers seem near rebellion against their elected officials. But so far these crises have not marked the end of consensual government. That is, however, not to downplay these often-perilous fault lines or the innate dangers to constitutional governments from military officers who assume political expertise and responsibilities well beyond military statutes and codes of conduct.

After all, Athens lost the war after Arginusae. Lincoln by August 1864 was attacked by generals on both sides of the battlefield, and contemporaries feared that the president's vision of an unconditional victory after that terrible summer was impossible. One reason Korea ended in stalemate was that key military decisions in late 1950–51 played out in public and were toxically politicized. A compliant Vietnam-era military that rarely voiced in-house objections through the chain of command to harebrained presidential directives helped to ensure a lethal deadlock in Vietnam, inevitable draft resistance at home, and eventually a humiliating flight from the Saigon embassy roof.

If the United States overcomes its tragic and mortifying defeat in Kabul, it will not be because brave and outspoken generals and admirals offered their resignations to make clear that their orders to abandon billions of dollars in military equipment, their own NATO allies, and loyal Afghans were unsound and dangerous and would disastrously weaken American deterrence and national security.

The United States is now well into its third century. It has and will experience existential crises in which civilians commit mayhem in the street and presidents ponder whether to send in federal troops, often gauging their decisions on political as well as security considerations. Careerist, compliant, and unimaginative officers will meekly carry out directives that they know will weaken the country, while outspoken and often unsteady generals and admirals will improperly enter the political fray in ways that they know exceed their statuary and traditional authority. And so far, the civilian–military relationship—and the nation—survive.

For all the talk of coups in 2017, there were none. Few chairmen of the Joint Chiefs will choose to follow General Milley's dangerous precedent of calling up his Chinese communist counterpart to voice his hunches that his own president is unstable.

A contested election passed from one party to another with a modicum of violence.

No president suspended habeas corpus or used the military to void an election or jail his predecessor.

In other words, in a time of a historic plague and the first national quarantine and lockdown in US history; a violent crisis in racial relations, with months of riots, arson, and looting; the White House grounds threatened; the Capitol stormed; and a president impeached twice (once as a private citizen), an often unsteady and uninspired military nevertheless largely obeyed civilian orders, and the unpopular and controversial presidents of both major parties did not order troops to attack their enemies.

Between 2017 and 2022 we may have come close to violating these sacred boundaries, but then again these have been unusual times, in which the military–civilian system and the tradition of legitimate civilian dissent were tested as rarely before and survived—if perhaps only barely so.

ABOUT THE CONTRIBUTORS

Victor Davis Hanson is the Martin and Illie Anderson Senior Fellow in Residence in Classics and Military History at the Hoover Institution. He is a nationally syndicated columnist for Tribune Media Services and the author of twenty-six books, most recently *The Dying Citizen*. Hanson is also the Wayne and Marcia Buske Distinguished Fellow in History, Hillsdale College, where he teaches courses in military history and classical culture. Among his honors are the Edmund Burke Award, the William F. Buckley Prize, the Bradley Prize, the National Humanities Medal, and the Claremont Institute's Statesmanship Award.

Peter R. Mansoor, colonel (ret.), US Army, is the General Raymond E. Mason Jr. Chair of Military History at the Ohio State University. Among other works, he is the author of *The GI Offensive in Europe: The Triumph of American Infantry Divisions, 1941–1945*; *Baghdad at Sunrise: A Brigade Commander's War in Iraq*; and *Surge: My Journey with General David Petraeus and the Remaking of the Iraq War*. His most recent publication is *The Culture of Military Organizations*, coedited with Williamson Murray.

Williamson Murray is a professor emeritus at the Ohio State University and Ambassador Anthony D. Marshall Professor Chair of Strategic Studies at Marine Corps University. He served in Southeast Asia with the US Air Force and has authored, coauthored, and edited a number of books, among which are *The Change in the European Balance of Power, 1938–1939*; *A War to Be Won: Fighting the Second World War*; *A Savage War: A Military History of the Civil War*; *Military Adaptation in War*; and *Military Innovation in the Interwar Period*.

Ralph Peters, a former US Army intelligence officer, strategic analyst, and prize-winning author, has published thirteen books with Civil War themes, as well as numerous other works of fiction and nonfiction on a broad range of topics. An essayist and former media commentator, he is currently at work on a song cycle dramatizing the history of the Pennsylvania anthracite fields.

Paul A. Rahe is the Roger and Martha Mertz Visiting Fellow in Classics at the Hoover Institution, Stanford University, and Charles O. Lee and Louise K. Lee Chair in the Western Heritage at Hillsdale College, where he is professor of history. He is the author or editor of numerous books, including *Republics Ancient and Modern: Classical Republicanism and the American Revolution* and, most recently, *Sparta's Second Attic War: The Grand Strategy of Classical Sparta, 446–418* BC. The University of Piraeus in Greece conferred on him its Themistocles Statesmanship Award in 2022.

Bruce S. Thornton is a research fellow at the Hoover Institution and an executive board member of its Role of Military History in Contemporary Conflict Working Group. He is the author of ten books and numerous essays, columns, articles, and reviews on Greek culture and civilization and their influence on Western civilization and on contemporary political and educational issues.

Bing West is a military historian who has written a dozen best-selling books about the wars in Vietnam, Iraq, and Afghanistan. His most recent books are *The Last Platoon: A Novel of the Afghanistan War* and, with coauthor General Jim Mattis, *Call Sign Chaos: Learning to Lead.* A graduate of Georgetown and Princeton Universities, where he was a Woodrow Wilson Fellow, he served in the US Marines infantry in Vietnam and later as assistant secretary of defense for international security affairs.

INDEX

Wool, John E., 39, 41
Working Group on Contemporary
 Conflict and Military History, 9
Worth, Cedric R., 52

Xenophon (historian)
 Arginusae Trial, 23, 28n12

Battle of Arginusae, 19–21, 27n5
 The Quick and the Dead, 22

Younger, Cole, 35

Zelensky, V., 101